Redemption: A Tale of Baseball and Life

By
Tom Miller

Table of Contents

Dedication

For Blondie

Prologue

I got beat by a four-eyed, fat bastard. It was a defeat that ruined a miraculous season and essentially ended my baseball career. While I realize this is a peculiar way to begin my story, it is an event I often think about. A game that occurred when I was just ten years old continues to be the bane of my existence some 53 years later.

It was the 1971 Rockville Boys Baseball Association's Pee Wee Championship Game. The best of three series was tied at a game apiece. My team, F.O. Day Construction, was just four outs away from victory. Our opponent was St. Mary's Elementary School, a traditional powerhouse and renowned cheater. But I will talk about that later.

By all rights, the inning should have already ended, but two routine groundballs booted by my second baseman had put the tying and go-ahead runs on base. A strikeout would end the threat and preserve our precarious 1-0 lead.

My pitch was almost perfect. A two-strike knee-high fastball painted black on the outside corner. I still don't know how the batter hit the ball. He certainly did not swing his bat. To this day, I am convinced his eyes were closed.

His feeble check swing and the sight of the ball lining over the head of my first baseman landing two inches in fair territory down the right field line is one that I still have nightmares about today. My initial thought was to strangle my second baseman. Would any of my teammates blame me?

I still recall the batter standing on third base after his two-out triple. His glasses were foggy. He clapped his hands loudly, stuck out his tongue, and gasped for breath. I doubt he had ever run that far in his life. Nevertheless, he was the hero, and I faced a one-run deficit. My left elbow throbbed in excruciating pain as the next batter approached the plate.

My name is Tom Miller, and I used to be a ballplayer.

Chapter 1
The Agony of Defeat

My athletic career had begun two years earlier as a third grader after I had joined the Cub Scouts. Rather than play in the Rockville Boys Baseball Association Minor League Division, my first experience with a team sport was fast-pitch softball. My team consisted of several members from my pack, all of us attending Twinbrook Elementary School. Our head coach was the father of one of my teammates who spent more time smoking Marlboro cigarettes than teaching us how to play.

Many of my teammates lacked any semblance of athletic ability. Most were more concerned with earning scouting badges than winning softball games. I, on the other hand, was probably the worst Cub Scout ever. I never learned to tie knots, pitch a tent, or perform any other duty expected of a typical scout. Hell, to this day, I cannot even hammer a nail straight.

Our opening game proved just how bad we were. Facing a pitcher who could bring heat, we were blasted 33-4. I provided our lone highlight when I smacked a grand slam late in the game.

I would be lying if I said we improved as the season progressed. Games would last forever because our pitchers had trouble throwing strikes. Back then, there was no such thing as the 10-run mercy rule. Instead, we suffered one long humiliating defeat after another. I played first base, so I had a front-row view of opponents scoring run after run after run.

One of our ugliest games occurred when we faced St. Mary's Elementary School (yep, those same bastards!) Trailing 29-2 in the final inning, I came to bat with the bases loaded. I drove a ball into the right-centerfield gap for a bases-clearing two-out double. As I pulled into second base, the St. Mary's shortstop took the throw from his outfielder and applied the tag to my leg as I was standing on the base. Even though I was called safe, the St. Mary's head coach argued with the umpire questioning the call. This, in turn, led to my head coach racing across the infield to challenge the St. Mary's coach to a fight. I continued to stand on second base, wondering if the lit cigarette dangling from the mouth of my coach would burn the face of the St. Mary's coach as they stood nose to nose. After some pushing and shoving and assorted language that I suspect would make the Pope blush, the game was called. The umpire feared someone was going to get hurt. Our two-out rally, cutting the lead to 25 runs, was robbed from us!

We finished the season with a record of 1-10. It was a

miracle that we won that single game. To celebrate our "successful" season, our den leaders organized a picnic. The highlight of the picnic was to be the Fathers vs. Sons softball game. It would prove to be an event that caused me much angst.

My father was not the most athletic person you would ever meet. He never played catch with me. He never taught me how to throw or hit. He never took me to sporting events. His idea of sports was fishing and watching The American Sportsman on ABC.

When I learned of the Father and Son game, I prayed that Dad would not attend. The last thing I wanted was to be teased at school because Dad could not play, or worse yet, played like a girl!

To my horror, not only did Dad show up, but he would also play second base! Luckily, I was the only left-handed batter on my team. So, when I came to the plate, I did my best not to hit the ball to him.

For five innings, I lived in fear of embarrassment. I was relieved when the game finally ended. Dad played well. He cleanly fielded the only ball hit to him and delivered a single in two at-bats. I could go to school on Monday with my reputation intact. Thanks, Dad!

Chapter 2
Family

I was born on September 25, 1960, at the US Naval Hospital in Bethesda, Maryland. My father was a Chief Hospital Corpsman, having served in the Navy since his high school graduation in 1943. Bethesda was his final duty station before his retirement in 1962. During his last two years in the Navy, he taught X-ray school to enlisted personnel. My mother would recall him coming home proud of himself for flunking half the class on an exam simply by changing a word or two on the practice test they had taken the day before. "They need to learn how to read," he would say. I suspect his students thought he was an asshole.

After serving nearly twenty years as a Navy corpsman, there was no doubt that Dad knew his stuff. One night while he had duty, my brothers Butch and Ted were playing chicken in the house, holding my sisters Cath and Barb on their shoulders. Barb soon fell to the floor with a resounding thud. Landing hard on her shoulder, she immediately burst into tears.

Mom ended up taking her to Bethesda Naval Hospital. Barb's doctor manipulated her arm and shoulder. He raised her arm above her head and pulled it this way and that. Barb remained stoic throughout this examination, not saying a word.

Reviewing Barb's X-rays, her doctor assured Mom that it was nothing to worry about, only a shoulder sprain.

Only upon returning to the car did Barb resume crying. "I didn't want to cry or say anything in front of the doctor," she told Mom.

Following a long and sleepless night for Barb and Mom, Dad returned home from work to find them at the front door. Mom demanded that they return to Bethesda so that Dad could take an X-ray himself.

Throughout the rest of her life, Mom would often say she had never seen Dad as angry as he was when his X-ray revealed a broken collarbone. He slammed the X-ray on the doctor's desk shouting, "What do you see here, Doc?" Dad was not someone to mess with.

Dad's naval career got off to an auspicious start. The day after his high school graduation, his father took him to the Navy Recruiting Office in Meadville, Pennsylvania. My grandfather was a longtime railroad mechanic. He desired to have his son follow in his footsteps and requested that he become a Machinist's Mate.

The recruiter was happy to oblige. However, he informed Dad that a Machinist's Mate rating would require a six-year obligation rather than the standard four. With no consultation whatsoever, my grandfather instructed Dad to sign the enlistment papers.

It was only after securing the signed paperwork that the recruiter informed them that the Navy had no vacancies for Machinist's Mates but urgently needed hospital corpsmen. Dad would be ordered to report to boot camp at the Great Lakes Naval Training Center in Illinois. Upon graduation, he would then attend Hospital Corps School for training to become a Navy corpsman. When Dad asked if he was still required to serve six years since there were no openings for Machinist's Mates, the recruiter responded, "You signed the paperwork, didn't you?"

I was the youngest of five. My two older brothers, Butch and Ted, were born in Meadville, and my two sisters, Barbara and Cathy, were born while Dad was stationed in Birmingham, Alabama. Mom's pregnancy in 1955 with Cathy proved extremely difficult. Requiring bed rest for a portion of her pregnancy, she was told by her Navy doctor that her fourth child would definitely be her last. I am told that she was not the least bit devastated by this news.

So imagine Mom's surprise five years later when she woke up several days in a row convinced she had morning sickness. Despite reassurances from Dad that her mind was just playing tricks on her, she finally convinced him that a trip to the Bethesda Naval Hospital was necessary.

Mom was shocked when told that she was indeed expecting, ironically by the very same Navy doctor who told her that her childbearing days were over. When reminded of their conversation and his diagnosis in 1955, his blunt response was simply, "Well, you win some, you lose some."

Despite my eventual discovery that I was an unplanned child (I like to think of myself as the miracle baby) I will always be grateful to Mom for instilling in me a love for sports. She grew up in Fort Wayne, Indiana, and played volleyball and basketball in high school. Mom loved baseball and often talked of watching her beloved Bob Feller pitch for the Cleveland Indians.

Later in life, she would fall asleep listening to the Baltimore Orioles on the radio. Her absolute passion was a hatred of the Washington Redskins and rooting against them on television, often with Dad sound asleep on the couch or reading one of his hundreds of paperback westerns.

When both Butch and Ted served as Navy corpsmen during the Vietnam War, it was Mom who played catch with me and later served as my bullpen catcher before games. She attended all of my games and was always my biggest fan. And it was Mom who convinced me that my fast-pitch softball career was over.

Chapter 3
Not a Great Start

When I signed up to play in the Rockville Boys Baseball Pee Wee League, teams were determined by the number of players from each elementary school. Since Twinbrook Elementary was one of the larger schools in Rockville; three teams typically represented the school. The Optimist Club was often the best of the three. Optimist usually contended for first place and typically consisted of the best players from the school.

The second team was sponsored by a local gas station, Leigh's Sunoco. They were often a fair to middling team that rarely posed a threat to the better teams in the league. It had been several years since they had won the city championship.

Finally, F.O. Day Construction sponsored the third Twinbrook team. No one could recall the last time they posted a winning record, they typically finished in last place. F.O. Day never beat good teams and was often nothing more than cannon fodder to superior teams like Optimist.

A lottery system chose all first-year players. In hindsight, I suspect that was pure bullshit. There was a reason why the best Twinbrook players ended up playing for Optimist and the average to poor players played for Leigh's and F.O. Day. The best players were scouted when they played in the Rockville Boys Minor League, and when the Pee Wee teams were chosen, they were conveniently slotted to the team that best matched their athletic ability.

St. Mary's Elementary was the only team not subjected to the draft lottery. Instead of fielding multiple teams, St. Mary's consisted of the best 9-10 players from their school. This was supposedly because they were a private school and had fewer students. Perhaps it was just a coincidence that all of their players were excellent ballplayers. As a result, they always contended for league titles. I called it cheating.

I was an unknown commodity since I had yet to play baseball. None of the Twinbrook coaches knew me, but I knew all of the Twinbrook players, and I was confident that I could compete against the best of them. Therefore, I was not surprised when F.O. Day drafted me.

Having just endured playing for a terrible fast-pitch softball team, F.O. Day proved no better. Simply put, we were just plain awful. We had few players who could hit, and our pitchers were even worse. One of our best players was a kid named Timmy Wise. He started the season as our starting catcher but quickly grew tired of trying to handle our pitching staff. None of our pitchers threw very hard or accurately. Timmy spent most of his time retrieving errant pitches from the backstop. It was only a short time before Timmy became our new starting pitcher.

Timmy was replaced by a big kid named Andy Thompson. At first glance, he would never strike one as being a ballplayer. Andy could not run worth a damn but soon proved to be one of our best hitters. Andy's defensive ability would come into focus the following year when we surprised everyone during our run to the city championship.

I started at first base, and while I never became the home run hitter I was when playing softball, I hit for a high average and drew my share of bases on balls. Timmy, Andy, and I became the core of the team and would have started for most other teams in the league. The lack of pitching and talent at other positions doomed us from the start.

Most of our games proved ugly affairs. Except for Timmy, none of our pitchers could consistently throw strikes. This resulted in long games where runs were typically generated by walks, hit batsmen, and wild pitches. By the middle of the season, our coaches began to use me as a pitcher. I was a tall kid and threw lefthanded. I looked as though I was a competent pitcher, but everything about the position was new to me. No one had ever shown me how to grip a baseball, how to hold runners on base, when to change speeds and other pitching nuances.

While I did not throw hard, I could throw strikes. Fewer walks and wild pitches made for quicker and lower-scoring games. However, wins continued to be hard to come by.

As our season passed the halfway mark, Mom started to experience health issues. Following many tests, doctors determined that she needed thyroid surgery. Admitted to the hospital on the night of one of my games, she was extremely upset about missing it. My sisters urged me to hit a home run for her. After failing in my first two at-bats, my chance to do so came down to my final plate appearance.

As I approached the batter's box, thoughts of Babe Ruth raced through my head. Should I point to the exact location where my mammoth home run would land? Should I take my time rounding the bases while thinking about my poor mother lying in her hospital bed? Would the crowd expect a curtain call?

The pitcher delivered a fastball down the middle of the plate, and I swung with all my might. The ball exploded off my bat. Never in my entire baseball career did I hit a ball harder. Unfortunately, rather than hitting the home run that Mom deserved, my line drive struck the pitcher on his right shoulder. He crumpled to the ground as the ball ricocheted toward the third baseman. I ran to first, and just as my foot hit the bag, the errant throw from the third baseman scooted past the first baseman. As I turned to run to second base, my cleat caught the edge of the bag, and I felt my right hamstring tear like paper. I fell to the ground, and my fingers dug into the dirt as intense pain shot through my leg. A stranger came out of the stands and bent down beside me. I can still remember the pungent stench of alcohol on his breath as he attempted to lift me to my feet. Suddenly, someone shoved him aside. It was Dad. After checking my leg for a possible fracture, he pulled me to my feet and helped me off the field.

I could barely walk to the car after the game ended. As an old Chief Hospital Corpsman, Dad said, "Walk on it. You'll be fine." As my family members walked ahead of me, I was convinced they would leave me stranded in the parking lot.

When we got home, I lay on the living room couch and eventually fell asleep. I awoke at 2 a.m. to a darkened, empty room. I had just dreamed that someone had murdered Dad and stuffed his body in the living room closet. I got to my feet and gently limped to the closet door. Each step proved excruciating. Tears rolled down my face as I had to see for myself the corpse in the closet. Just as I opened the door, Dad came out of the bedroom to investigate the noise I was making. "Dad! You're alive!" I screamed. He simply shook his head and told my dumb ass to go to bed.

My injury proved season-ending. My torn hamstring would cause me to miss the final eight games. We finished the season with a dismal 4-24 record. I would have to wait until next season to reunite with my teammates while hoping new players would replace many of them. But it would be my coaches who I would miss the most. They were not like other coaches in the league. They were not popular but were undoubtedly the most honorable. I have always remembered them.

Chapter 4
A Nation at War

A typical Rockville Pee Wee baseball coach was in his mid-40s, living an upper-middle-class life in one of the wealthiest counties in America. Many were lawyers, doctors, and white-collar professionals. Since Washington, D.C. was located just a short drive on the Beltway, many coaches were federal employees. The one constant between most coaches was that their rosters included their own child.

F.O. Day coaches were not your stereotypical ones. None were older than 23. None were married. None had kids. All possessed long hair, mustaches, or beards. While most teams were led by a single manager, F.O. Day sometimes had as many as five coaches in the dugout at the same time.

All of our coaches had been childhood friends. All were 1967 graduates of Richard Montgomery High School. As the Vietnam War raged in Southeast Asia, these friends made the life-altering decision to enlist in the United States Marine Corps following their graduation. Taking advantage of the USMC's "Buddy Program," eleven of these friends enlisted together and reported to Parris Island, South Carolina, for Marine Corps boot camp. They would all eventually wind up in South Vietnam.

A photograph was taken of the group on August 24, 1967, at Fort Holabird in Baltimore, waiting for their flight to Savannah, Georgia, and subsequent bus trip to Parris Island. The clean-cut individuals were the perfect image of youthful innocence. Their smiles expressed complete confidence. Their eyes beamed with hope and desire to serve their country.

A couple of years later, a similar photograph was taken. A reunion was held among these same friends, but only eight were present. One had been killed in action. Two were still in the Marine Corps. Most of them had been wounded in battle. Our head coach, Wayne Kline, had suffered a severe head injury, which required the planting of a steel plate in his head. Wayne would be assisted by some of his Marine Corps buddies. One coach had received shrapnel in his back after a fellow soldier had stepped on a boobytrap. He would often pitch batting practice shirtless, his scarred back, a reminder to the rest of us of his pain and suffering. Only two of the eleven friends came home with no physical injuries. One of them, Butch Gavin, lost his leg in a motorcycle accident shortly after his discharge from the Marine Corps.

Dad, having served in the Pacific in World War II, did not know what to make of my coaches. During this time, Walter Cronkite would announce the number of U.S. service member's deaths on the nightly news. Anti-war demonstrations swept the nation. Dad criticized those demonstrators who marched against the war and burned their draft cards in public acts of defiance. As our season progressed, Dad's attitude about the war changed. My coaches always showed respect to him. I suspect that initially, it was simply a continuation of the respect U.S. Marines show to the corpsmen who share their battlefield. As Dad got to know them, he understood their sacrifices for our country. Dad came to realize that Vietnam was not like the war he experienced. Vietnam drove a stake between America's youth and the U.S. establishment. Dad loved our nation, but he criticized the war as time passed. I am proud to say that my coaches helped him change his mind.

Unfortunately, our coaches never gained the respect of our opponents. They were virtually shunned by other coaches in the league. Whether it was because of differences in physical appearance or our eventual success, there was always an air of tension at our games. Opposing coaches, their players, and their fans would call our coaches "hippies," "druggies," and worse yet, "draft dodgers." Somehow, to the credit of our coaches, these comments were always ignored.

July 4th marked the halfway point of our season. The annual All-Star Game would be played at Woodley Gardens Park in Rockville. During my first year, Timmy and I were chosen to represent F.O. Day in this game. When I arrived for our first practice, the head coach of the team said, "Oh, you play for the hippies. Tell those assholes to cut their hair."

During my first year of playing Pee Wee baseball, both my team and our coaches were laughed at and looked down upon by other teams. F.O. Day had long been the laughingstock of the league. All of that would change during the 1971 season.

Chapter 5
A New Season

As I entered my second season of Pee Wee baseball, several changes occurred to the F.O. Day roster. Gone were most of the pitching staff from the previous year. That is what is typically termed today as "addition by subtraction." Hopefully, we would no longer experience two-hour-plus games in which our opponents could pile up runs without even having to swing a bat. Timmy would be our starting pitcher, and I would be his backup.

While I preferred playing first base, my pitching experience from the previous season enabled me to gain the confidence that I could do the job. Having Andy as our full-time catcher helped instill confidence in all of us.

We were scheduled to play two games a week, each game lasting five innings. The season started in May and would continue through August. Teams who qualified for the playoffs would play into September. Pitchers were limited to ten innings per week. There was no such thing as pitch counts, so barring injury, Timmy would be doing the bulk of the pitching.

The key addition to our team was a short kid named David Moody. He had long hair and bore a striking resemblance to

Davy Jones of The Monkees. He was one of the better athletes at Twinbrook Elementary. Like me, David had not played Minor League ball. I had played other sports against him and knew that he would be a welcome addition to our team. His best sport was duck pin bowling. How cool was that? He was known to bowl 150-point games routinely.

David had nearly decided not to play baseball in order to concentrate on his bowling game. We were fortunate when he decided to give baseball a try. David would be our starting shortstop when Timmy pitched and would move to third base when I took the mound. He proved to be an outstanding fielder, and if Gold Gloves were awarded, he would have easily been our team's recipient.

The other positive addition was Jerry "Duck" Gavin. He was the kid brother of one of our coaches from the previous year. He was a good hitter, but most importantly, he was our only outfielder who could routinely catch a fly ball.

Other players on the team included Davey Richardson, a second baseman who indeed could be described as "all hit and no field." Simply put, this kid could not catch a cold. Johnny Jackson and Marty Jones manned the outfield next to Duck. Both had played the previous year in the Minor League without much playing action, so it was no surprise that the lottery system had assigned them to us. Eddie Shuster would play first base when I pitched. He could not hit worth a damn, but could at least catch a ball thrown to him. Our final player was Joey Mitchell. He rode our bench but was a friendly kid. His biggest talent was always being first in line for post-game snacks and refreshments.

Wayne returned as our head coach. He still had his long hair and continued to be disrespected by other coaches and fans. After a couple of practices, I think Wayne began to share our optimism. David anchored our infield defense, and it had become quite clear Andy would be one of the best catchers in the league. Could we double our win total from the previous year?

Opening day was just around the corner. We were excited to get the season started.

Chapter 6
Opening Day

Our opening-day opponent was Leigh's Sunoco. Since we both attended the same school, all the players knew each other. Leigh's had finished the previous season with 12 wins and 12 losses. Another season of mediocrity.

As a bonus, our opening game was set for under the lights at Dogwood Park. Night games typically drew larger crowds, and during the early part of the season, other coaches would attend to scout future opponents.

Leigh's began the game like a house afire. They scored eight runs in the first two innings against Timmy. While successfully throwing strikes and limiting walks, Timmy was surrendering hit after hit. Somewhat shockingly, we did not wither under Leigh's early onslaught. After scoring a single run in the bottom of the first, we exploded for seven more in the second. The game was tied 8-8, entering the top of the third.

Wayne told me to take the mound to start the inning as we took the field. Even though we were tied, I suspect the number of solid hits surrendered by Timmy resulted in Wayne's decision for a pitching change. I took the mound for my warmups, a bit surprised that my pitching debut had occurred so soon. Mom and Dad were in the stands watching me. More importantly, so was Butch.

Butch had missed my previous year, completing his final year in the Navy. As a result, this would be the first time he had ever seen me play. After completing a couple of warm-up tosses I heard a voice from the bleachers, "I sure hope you can throw faster than that!" Big Brother was just getting started.

After my third warmup pitch, the same voice cried again, "Boy, you suck! Where did you learn how to pitch?" Many people in the bleachers began to laugh. Even worse, so did many of my classmates on both teams.

Butch had embarrassed me in front of my friends and teammates. I was pissed! I threw my final warmup pitch as hard as I could. Andy's mitt smacked loudly as my pitch was a perfect strike.

My anger had not subsided as the first batter approached the plate. I threw the ball hard again with the same result. The batter swung meekly at my next pitch. Andy did not have to move his mitt as I struck out the batter on my third pitch. After a ground out to David and my second strikeout of the inning, we entered the bottom of the third, still tied at 8.

Andy opened our half of the inning with a long homer to left. Timmy's bases-clearing triple resulted in three more runs, upping our lead to 12-8. In the top of the fourth, I struck out two more batters, and after scoring seven more runs in the bottom of the inning, our victory was near.

I pitched another shutout inning to close the game. The final score was 19-8. I finished the game with seven strikeouts in three innings. I was unsure who was more surprised about my performance, Wayne, or the coaches in the stands. I guess I should give some credit to Butch. He had brought out the best of me. My newly discovered fastball had opened eyes. Nevertheless, I was content to leave the pitching to Timmy. But things were about to change.

Chapter 7
Big Bro #1

Butch was the best athlete I have ever seen. Before enlisting in the Navy, he had worked part-time for a company called Flow Laboratories in Rockville. Dad began to work there upon his retirement from the Navy. All of my siblings would eventually work there too. Butch played on the Flow softball team and was their best player. He could run, throw, and hit for power. Butch was also an outstanding left fielder who caught everything hit his way. No one dared to challenge his throwing arm. And softball was not even his best sport.

Butch attended the same high school as my coaches. Richard Montgomery was a high school football powerhouse. Its most famous alum, Mike Curtis, went on to be named All-Pro during a distinguished NFL playing career. During the years Butch attended the school, Richard Montgomery experienced two undefeated seasons and enjoyed a 26-game winning streak. Its head coach, Roy Lester, was a coaching legend. Following another undefeated season in 1968, he was named head football coach at the University of Maryland, quite an accomplishment for a high school coach.

Lester would scout future players by visiting junior high schools in Rockville. He would have the physical education teachers schedule outdoor touch football games on the days he visited. It was during his visit to Broome Junior High, he first saw Butch throw a football. Immediately after class, Lester approached Butch and told him that he expected Butch to be his new starting quarterback. When reminded that his current quarterback was just a junior, Lester replied "That's okay; he'll be my new running back when you join the team."

Butch was a tall and skinny kid, 6'2", 165 lbs, by the time he entered high school. In gym class when playing touch football, he teamed up with his best friend, Bobby Dotson. Their calls were never too fancy. Bobby, who could run like a deer, would go long, and Butch would complete 50-yard passes to him. Despite pleas from Lester to go out for the team, Butch never showed any interest. He and Bobby preferred calling out sick once a week and miraculously recovering in time to play on the new billiards table my parents had purchased over the summer.

Butch and Bobby got into their fair share of trouble. Both were kicked off their school bus for dropping chains outside the rear exit of the bus to watch sparks fly on the pavement. Ted recalls the time when they nearly caught the woods on fire next to Broome Junior High. Butch and Bobby had skipped school that day. Ted was in gym class and saw them chasing a groundhog. Once the groundhog escaped into its hole, one of them had the brilliant idea to smoke it out. They stuffed the hole with dry leaves and set a fire. Soon, the fire began to spread. As they ran away, Bobby shouted, "Damn Miller, we done caught the woods on fire!" Luckily the fire department arrived in time to save the woods. Whatever became of the groundhog remains a mystery.

Lester was especially pissed watching Butch and Bobby embarrass his varsity players during gym classes. No one could throw as far or as accurately as Butch. His talent was unquestionable. Over the years, I have often wondered if Butch regrets not playing for Lester. He would have been a star.

When I was in high school and for years afterward, my friends and I would play Butch and Ted's buddies in tackle football every Sunday morning. Games would start promptly at 10 a.m. and be over before the NFL games kicked off. These games got rough. It is amazing none of us killed each other. Our strategy when playing against Butch was pretty simple. Whenever Butch had the ball, we needed to gang-tackle him to bring him down, for not only was Butch a great passer but a powerful runner, too.

I will never forget the time when Butch was dragging two of my teammates toward the goal line. I joined the tackle by grabbing him around his shoulders, but in doing so, my hand accidentally hit him in the nose. 'You better watch it, Tommy" was all he said as he returned to his huddle. I later learned that in their huddle, Butch told his teammates, "Just give me the damn ball!"

I cannot recall too much about what happened next. I just remember Butch running straight at me. His left knee slammed into my right shoulder, knocking me on my ass. As I tried to comprehend if my collarbone was still intact, his right cleat stepped on my chest as he walked into the endzone. My left shoulder was bruised with all the colors of a rainbow, and I could not lift my arm for weeks.

During the late '70s, tennis became the new craze throughout the United States. I would often play with classmates or friends from my part-time job at a local movie theatre. I never became a very good tennis player, but that did not stop me from challenging Butch to a match. I finally found a sport in which he did not excel. And being the obnoxious baby brother, I relished the opportunity to give him grief across the net. Unfortunately, our match lasted less than 15 minutes. That's how long it took for Butch to fling his racket over the fence, get in his car, and drive home. He never played tennis again.

It was a successful start to a new season. Defeating Leigh's had given us confidence. I was happy that Butch was home. I hoped he would come to more games. I just wanted to make certain he had no reason to embarrass me again.

Chapter 8
Winning Streak

My teammates and I could not wait to attend school the following day. It was a rare occurrence when an F.O. Day player could brag about being undefeated. We had stomped Leigh's pretty good. No one on Optimist seemed impressed. But then again, Optimist players were used to winning.

Our second game was played on the following Saturday afternoon. Our opponent was G.C. Murphy's department store. Their starting pitcher threw hard but was very wild. We scored several runs to start the game as he could not find the plate. He was removed from the game after plunking Timmy in the rib cage. His replacement faired no better.

When Timmy took the mound to pitch the bottom of the first, it became immediately apparent that he was hurting. After seeing Timmy grimmace while throwing his warmup pitches, Wayne made a pitching change. I took the ball and began to throw hard once again. I guess my focus from the previous season to throw strikes had helped me to develop successful pitching mechanics. Having Andy give me a large target behind the plate also helped.

We won our second straight game 14-1. I pitched a complete

game, allowing only a couple of hits while striking out 11. We were only two wins away from matching our win total from the previous season. But we suspected Optimist still needed to be impressed.

Our next game would be our first actual test. Our opponent, Twinbrook Deli, also started the season 2-0. I was familiar with a couple of their players, having been teammates of them during last year's All-Star game. They were pretty good.

To my surprise, Wayne informed me at our practice before the game that I would be the starting pitcher. I became nervous with anticipation. While warming up before the start of the game, Ted and a couple of his coworkers from Flow arrived to watch us play. With Butch sitting in the stands with Mom and Dad, I now had two brothers waiting to give me grief.

I started the game on a somewhat shaky note. I walked the lead-off batter but was bailed out when Andy gunned him down when he attempted to steal second base. After walking the second batter, Andy's pickoff throw to first base eliminated that threat as well. Andy had quickly become our secret weapon in a league where most teams tried to be aggressive on the basepaths. From that point onward, few teams dared to test his arm.

I eventually settled down, and we won the game 10-0. I pitched a complete game shutout and finished with ten strikeouts. We were now 3-0 and flying high. And we could care less if Optimist was impressed or not.

Chapter 9
Big Bro #2

Ted was fortunate to survive childhood. While walking home from Sunday school with Butch in Portsmouth, Virginia, Ted ran across the street and was hit by a car. Butch recalls Ted putting his arms out like he was Superman in a futile attempt to stop the vehicle before impact. Ted was run over and spun down the street like a top, fracturing his skull and breaking his leg in the process.

Butch ran home and cried, "Ted's dead!" to Grandma Schultz, who was taking care of our family while Mom was in the Portsmouth Naval Hospital recovering from surgery.

Dad arrived at the emergency room when ER personnel were examining Ted. While removing his clothing, they found a glob of cooked spinach in one pocket of his Sunday school jacket and chunks of cooked liver in the other. A common ploy by Ted was to stuff offensive foods at dinner into his pockets to be discarded later. Apparently, he had not had an opportunity to do so the night before because Grandma made him take off his jacket before going out to play. When she heard about these surprising findings, she cried, "I'll never make him eat liver or spinach again." Ted would later explain that he wore his Sunday school jacket all the time when outside playing Cowboys. He thought it looked cool to have his belt and holster over his jacket like Bat Masterson on TV.

Butch laughs about this incident to this day- how funny it was that Ted could think he could put out his arms and stop a car and how he spun around and around in the street. Ted always responds, "You had one job to do, get your five-year-old little brother to and back from Sunday school safely. You fucked up."

A brief mention of other Butch and Ted incidents:

- After watching a Three Stooges television episode, Butch cracked open Ted's head by hitting him with an RC bottle. Butch was surprised that the bottle didn't shatter like it did in the Three Stooges program. Ted was off to the hospital for stitches.

- Butch found a box of discarded old phonograph records. He tossed one, unknowingly inventing the first frisbee, which flew gracefully through the air before striking Ted in the head and smashing into pieces. Ted was off to the hospital for stitches.

- After watching Disney's The Legend of Sleepy Hollow, Ted and Butch went out with neighborhood kids to play tag. Butch made Ted "It" and told him to zip up his jacket over his head so he would look headless. That would make the game more fun! Ted did so and promptly ran into a laundry pole. He was off to the hospital for more stitches. When Mom arrived at the Portsmouth Naval Hospital, the senior corpsman on duty recognized her from earlier in the week when she brought Ted in for stitches after the record-throwing accident and said, "Mrs. Miller, it's too early to take your son's stitches out. We said to come back in seven days." Mom responded, "I know. We're here for some new ones."

- Butch and some friends were walking alongside railroad tracks. They picked up some rocks and challenged who could throw one over some trees that were lining the tracks. Butch heaved one over, and they heard a scream. He had hit Ted in the head with the rock. Fortunately, no trip to the hospital was needed. Dad applied a butterfly bandage.

- When traveling with Butch, Ted, Barb, and Cath from Birmingham to join Dad at his new duty station at Portsmouth. Mom stopped at a Howard Johnson's Restaurant (probably just to take a short rest and have the kids use the bathroom since there was never any money for eating out). Butch and Ted ran around and around the building playing tag. Somebody had dropped an ice cream cone on the sidewalk at one end of the building. Butch deftly jumped over it. Ted did not, causing him to slip and fall into the brick wall opening a huge gash over his left eye. Off to a hospital for stitches. On this same trip, the night before, the kids were jumping from bed to bed in a motel room. While Barb was in midair, Butch kicked the beds farther apart, causing Barb to dive into the metal bed frame face-first. Off to the hospital for stitches. When Mom finally arrived in Portsmouth after a harrowing and exhausting trip with four kids and a dog, Dad asked, "What took you so long?"

- While living in Portsmouth, Butch and Ted formed the Dare Devil Club with their best friend, Butch Brewer. One wintry day Ted was dared to walk across an ice-covered portion of the Great Dismal Swamp. He took two small and tentative steps and proceeded to fall through the thin ice, forcing brother Butch to jump in to save him. Ted still doesn't know how they didn't succumb to hypothermia on their long walk home.

- The Dare Devil Club thought it would be funny to stuff and dress a dummy, then hang it by a rope over a branch dangling over a dimly lit neighborhood street. When cars would come by, they would release their hold on the rope to allow the dummy to come swinging down in front of them. All was fun and games until one poor woman slammed her brakes and exited her car screaming hysterically, believing that she had just witnessed a hanging and had run over the body.

- Butch and Butch Brewer once lowered Ted down onto a railroad bridge trestle about 40 feet above the Elizabeth River. They then lowered themselves down to join him. While they were able to hoist and pull themselves back up, Ted, smaller and three years younger, could not. Repeated attempts to reach and grab him to pull back up failed, chiefly because Ted was scared shitless of heights and was certain that he would be dropped to the river far below. Ted's fellow Dare Devil Club members then deserted him as they ran home to get help. They returned with Dad and Mr. Brewer. Needless to say, Dad was pissed. He and Mr. Brewer leaned over and stretched their hands out to Ted but he refused to grab them over and over again, fearful that they would drop him too. After much cajoling and ultimately a threat of a beating by Dad, Ted allowed them to grasp his hands and pull him up.

Ted is the jokester in the family. Everyone has long known to never sit next to him during a wedding or a funeral. He can make one laugh at the most inopportune moment. Celebrity deaths are his specialty. He often sends sick jokes about the deceased within a few hours of his or her demise.

Ted was also a practical joker. Without a doubt, the greatest practical joke he ever played occurred on a Sunday morning before one of our tackle football games. I agreed to meet him before any of the other players arrived. Ted brought a liter of sterilized pig blood from Flow. The blood was contained in a thick plastic bag, which we proceeded to tape to my chest under my jersey. When all the other players arrived and the game began, I started to taunt Ted. "You can't cover me! You're too slow." I went out for a pass with Ted following close behind. Just as the pass arrived, Ted shoved me to the ground. I screamed in pain as I tried to tear the blood bag. As players began to approach me, I cried out that I had landed on a piece of glass. Finally able to puncture the bag with my fingers, blood splattered everywhere as they rolled me over.

My brother-in-law Bill turned ghostly white. I was certain he was about to puke. My theatre buddy Dave screamed out, "He needs medical attention!" The prank lasted a few more seconds until someone heard the bag crinkle. I just wish we had it on film!

Ted is also extremely good at setting up someone to watch horrible movies. He will rave about a movie, telling everyone that they must watch it. And once they do, they realize what a clunker or letdown it actually is. He convinced Butch to go see Escape from New York by claiming you got to see Adrienne Barbeau's magnificent bare breasts. Ted told him there was a scene in the movie where the camera slowly pans from her bare back around to her front, where it focuses on her humongous naked boobs. There is indeed such a scene. You do see her bare back as the camera slowly pans around to the front, where you see her face. Sucker!

One time Ted convinced Barb and me to go see a midnight showing of Eraserhead. It is now a cult classic, but we absolutely hated it. It's definitely one of the most awful and weirdest movies I have ever seen. Ted will argue we were just too young to appreciate the greatness of this surreal art film with its erotic imagery and nightmarish take on the perils of fatherhood and understand how it unshackles suppressed thoughts and questions the meaning of life itself. He will only grudgingly admit that we should have been stoned to have fully appreciated this extraordinary masterpiece.

Ted is one of the most competitive persons I've known. He hates to lose at anything! Playing board games with him when we were younger was an absolute nightmare. Whether it was Monopoly, Risk, or Stratego, as long as he was winning, you were not allowed to quit the game. But if Ted was losing, it would be only a matter of time before he flipped the board sending pieces flying everywhere.

One of my favorite board games was Broadside, a Revolutionary War naval battle game. The game consisted of an attacking force pitted against ships on the defensive, guarding merchant ships moored in a harbor. The offensive ships were painted blue and consisted of more ships and sails than the red, defensive forces. The harbor was guarded by mines and land-based batteries of cannons. There were four cannons, two marked on the bottom as either "hit" or "miss".

The mines were marked either as "pass" or "sink." Attacking ships would lose sails if hit by cannon fire or sink if struck by mines. Ted always wanted to be the attacking force. He had the uncanny ability to pass over mines marked "pass" and enter the harbor past cannons marked "miss." He was able to do this time and time again. It was absolutely unbelievable and utterly frustrating to me how he never lost ships to mine sinkings or ship sails to cannon fire.

I could NEVER beat Ted at this game! It was only years later that Ted finally confessed that he had secretly marked the tips of "pass" mines and barrel ends of "miss" cannons with a magic marker. Cheating bastard!

Ted and his coworkers began to attend more of my games. I think they were even becoming impressed with our success. Our next game would be against Ernie's Pizza. We were looking to match our win total from the previous season, but the game would prove we had dents in our armor. Was our success premature, or worse, a bit exaggerated?

Chapter 10
Frustration

The game versus Ernie's Pizza proved to be one of utter frustration. Once again, I was chosen to be the starting pitcher, and while I was able to keep them scoreless through three innings, our offense sputtered. A couple of walks and subsequent stolen bases put our runners in scoring position, but we failed to deliver a timely hit.

In the top of the fourth, I struck out the first two batters, then gave up a flyball to left field. Marty camped under the ball but allowed it to hit off the heel of his glove. By the time he recovered the dropped ball the Ernie's batter had reached second base. The next batter proceeded to hit a slow ground ball to second base, which Davey watched travel through his legs for another two-out error. We trailed 1-0 entering the bottom of the fourth.

Victory seemed within our grasp in the bottom of the fourth when we loaded the bases with no outs. But then, inexplicably, Davey swung on a 3-0 pitch and popped up to third. Marty then took a called third strike. Finally, Duck grounded out to short to end our threat. We continued to trail by a single run entering the final inning.

Ernie's leadoff batter started the fifth inning with a bunt, which Andy proceeded to throw into right field. This error was just the start of the onslaught of mistakes that were to come. Before the inning was over; three more errors contributed to a 4-0 Ernie's lead. Andy hit a home run in the bottom of the inning, but we lost 4-1. I had pitched another complete game, striking out nine while surrendering three hits. What bothered me the most was issuing two bases on balls, with both ending up costing us a run.

Our record now stood at three wins and one defeat. Our confidence had taken a hit. The question was how we would respond? In three days, we would take on E.J. Korvette. Could we get back on the winning track?

Chapter 11
Let's Roll

Following our first season loss, we caught a bunch of flak at school. Optimist remained undefeated, and Leigh's Sunoco had evened their record at 2-2. Could we become the best Twinbrook team? The game against E.J. Korvette would go a long way in determining whether we were contenders or pretenders.

Compared to other teams, F.O. Day's practices were unusual. We practiced on the Twinbrook Elementary ballfield, one that formed gulleys and potholes in the infield each time it rained. You risked losing teeth if you tried to field a ground ball. And if you tried running the bases, you could snap your ankle if you stepped into one of its many holes.

Dad had approached the Mayor of Rockville the year before at the All-Star Game to complain about the poor field conditions. To the Mayor's credit, two large trucks appeared a couple of days later to dig up and smooth out our playing field. Unfortunately, this cosmetic repair only lasted until the next rain. The gulleys and potholes would appear all over again. We were screwed. We were stuck practicing on a shitty field.

Our practices simply consisted of batting practice. Wayne

would pitch to one batter at a time, while the rest of us stayed in the relatively safe confines of the outfield. Once everyone hit, we would have a second round of batting practice, or Wayne would hit fungos into the outfield. We never took infield practice, and since Timmy and David provided stellar defense at shortstop and third base, I suspect Wayne felt that infield practice was not necessary. Perhaps if we had a better field to practice on; regular infield practice would have helped Davey at second base. Heaven knows he needed all the practice he could get.

The game vs. E.J. Korvette was one of the best games we played all year. Simply put, we kicked the living crap out of them. Everyone in our lineup got a hit and scored a run. Even Joey got some playing time but was upset about losing his place in the post-game snack and beverage line. Things got so out of control that when we batted in the fourth inning, Wayne instructed Andy to strike out on purpose so the game would end quicker. I pitched a complete game shutout with 12 strikeouts.

Over the next three games, we became an offensive juggernaut. Everyone seemed to find their hitting stroke, and we ran wild on the basepaths. None of the games were close, and I continued to be our starting pitcher. Even when we got huge leads, Wayne refused to change pitchers. He was committed to riding the hot hand until our fortunes changed. My arm began to hurt following games, but after applying ice and heat, the pain would usually disappear.

Our record now stood at seven wins and one defeat. We were tied for first place with Optimist following their surprising defeat to Leigh's. We knew our chance to finally defeat Optimist had come. Sole possession of first place was on the line. And they were our next opponent.

Chapter 12
What a Crappy Way to Lose!

Due to an earlier postponement, a makeup game was scheduled two days before we faced Optimist. Instead of playing our regular two games per week, the Optimist game would be our third. I had pitched a complete five-inning game earlier in the week, and three innings of our blowout win vs. Rockville Elks. Before that game, Mom questioned our coaches about the ten-innings per-week pitching rule. Should I even pitch that game? Shouldn't I be saved for the Optimist game? Wayne assured her everything was fine. He said a new weekly accumulation of innings would begin on Saturday for the Optimist game.

A large crowd gathered for our big game. Even one of Twinbrook's 6th grade teachers, Mr. Smith, was there. To put it bluntly, the man scared the hell out of me. I thanked God that he was not my teacher. Kids in his class routinely experienced his wrath. If a student was not paying attention, they were subject to being struck by a thrown beanbag. Later that school year Mr. Smith would break a student's leg in the Faculty vs. Student soccer game. The man was unhinged.

One day, my class was playing Mr. Smith's class in basketball during recess. When the whistle blew for us to return to class, a couple of us took the opportunity to dunk a few times on a seven foot rim. Mr. Smith, always a bit of a showoff, told us to stop and he would demonstrate the proper way to perform a 360-degree dunk. Nearly six feet tall, he jumped into the air while cradling the basketball in his right hand. Unfortunately, his head hit one of the metal hooks on the rim, where the net should have been attached to. As he landed, blood started splurting from a hole in his head. It was one of the funniest things I had ever witnessed. Knowing he would have beaten my ass to a pulp if he saw me laughing. I turned my head to prevent him from seeing me do so.

Optimist had one of the best pitchers in the league. Jimmy Brett threw hard and had excellent control. I looked forward to our matchup. The large crowd added to the excitement. Brett started the game, retiring our first two batters. Batting third, I fouled off several tough pitches before working a base on balls, I immediately stole second and third. I was stranded there after the Optimist center fielder made a great running catch on a hard hit by Andy.

In the bottom of the first, Brett hit a sinking line drive to left, which skidded between Marty's legs allowing Brett to reach second base. The next batter blooped a single to right to drive in the game's first run. I escaped further damage by striking out the next three batters.

We stranded a couple of runners in the top of the second inning and again in the third. We were confident that we would eventually break through. We certainly were not intimidated by our opponent. In the meantime, I breezed through the second inning, retiring all three batters on bunt attempts. By not trying to swing the bat, I felt Optimist might be the one feeling a bit intimidated.

As I began pitching in the bottom of the third, I noticed the Optimist coaches gathered next to their dugout. After I proceeded to strike out the first batter, the Optimist head coach approached the home plate umpire. The umpire then told Wayne to bring his scorebook to him. After a few minutes of discussion, Wayne tossed his scorebook against the backstop. The umpire had just awarded a forfeit victory to Optimist because I had just exceeded my ten-innings-per-week pitch limit. I felt like I had been gut-punched. I slowly walked off the mound while the Optimist players celebrated their victory. To lose in that manner was simply devastating. I walked to our station wagon and sat in the back seat. I did not want anyone to see me crying.

We learned that before the game, the Optimist scorekeeper approached Wayne's girlfriend, our scorekeeper, and asked to see our scorebook. She did not realize he counted the innings I had pitched that week. The Optimist manager knew when I would exceed the ten-inning limit. When I struck out the first batter in the third inning, he appealed to the umpire.

Our scorekeeper was heartbroken. She felt it was her fault that we lost. Mom was ready to strangle Wayne. She had been right all along. Not knowing the rules had just cost us a big game.

Wayne apologized to us at our next practice. He accepted responsibility for our loss. He hoped we would get another chance to play Optimist. We all did.

Chapter 13
They Would Eat Anything

I never like to lose, even when playing for bad teams when losses were inevitable. After any loss, I just wanted to be left alone. I would sulk for an hour or two, replaying the game over and over in my head. What did I do wrong? What could I have done better? After a while, I would grab my glove and a hard rubber ball and bounce it off the steps of my house. I would pretend I was pitching for the Pittsburgh Pirates, making throw after throw against the steps, pitching against Brooks Robinson, Harmon Killebrew, and others. Some days, I would spend hours lost in my fantasy baseball world.

The loss against Optimist just felt different. I thought we were the better team and that our victory was stolen. Never mind that Wayne had screwed up. Never mind that I had indeed exceeded my weekly innings limit. We had lost a game decided by rules. Not by which team was better.

To cheer me up, Mom promised to make me my favorite dinner, chicken parmigiana with extra cheese, mushrooms, and noodles. Barb and Cathy were thrilled with my dinner selection because, trust me, dinners in the Miller household could be a bit "unusual."

Simply put, my parents would eat anything. I guess being Depression Era kids had something to do with that. There was absolutely nothing either of them would not eat. You knew you were in trouble when Dad would announce, "It tastes like chicken," as Mom served the nightly mystery dinner.

One summer, I remember visiting Mom's family in Fort Wayne, Indiana. Her relatives lived on a large farm. Dad grabbed a flashlight and fishing rod that night and walked out the door. I followed him to a pond and watched him shine the flashlight on large, unsuspecting bullfrogs. He dangled his lure in front of a frog, causing it to hook itself. After catching a full basket, we returned to the house. I followed Dad into the kitchen and watched in horror as he chopped off frogs' legs left and right. The kitchen counter looked like a crime scene. It was a sight that would traumatize most 5-year-olds, myself included. Who was Dad kidding? Did he actually think I would eat one once he had cooked them? Tastes like chicken, my ass!

Another time, Dad returned from fishing at Great Falls with a giant snapping turtle. It smelled putrid! I had no idea what he planned to do with the turtle until he dangled a screwdriver in front of its mouth. The turtle swiftly clamped onto the screwdriver while Dad pulled the tool towards him. This resulted in the turtle's neck being extended and exposed to the sharp knife Dad held in his other hand. The beheading took place in front of me, and a couple of my neighborhood friends. We watched in horror as Dad placed the lifeless turtle in a large pot. Turtle soup was on the menu for the night. Our kitchen smelled like death. I cannot imagine what my friends told their parents.

Butch remembers the time our family drove from Birmingham, Alabama, to Detroit. Dad prepared soup for the trip. When they stopped for lunch, Ted complained there were small bugs floating in his soup. "Stop your whining. Just eat it; they won't harm you," Dad said. Butch said they only had the soup, kool-aid, and fig newtons for the entire trip.

Cathy is still traumatized by coming home from school one day to find a dead baby calf sprawled across the kitchen table. She still vividly recalls Dad carving it up piece by piece. What really gave her nightmares was watching him slice off its tongue, calling it a delicacy.

While Dad did the majority of cooking in our house, Mom was prone to prepare her own fair share of inedible dinners. Mom once spent most of her day preparing shrimp creole. The smell radiating from the kitchen was revolting. I have never been inside a crematorium, but I am certain its aroma must be similar to the dinner that Mom was cooking.

Fortunately, Mom and Dad ate at the kitchen table that night while us kids ate in the living room. None of us could eat more than one bite. The flavor of the shrimp dish was even worse than its odor. Even our family dog, Salty, refused our offers of a free meal. Ted resorted to his favorite ploy and stuffed his pants pockets with the unsavory serving. The rest of us scraped our portions into a paper bag. We hid the bag in the living room closet until the coast was clear to dispose it in the garbage.

I was thankful for Mom fixing me my favorite meal. One recognized by normal families. I wanted to get back on the field and put the memory of the Optimist loss behind us. The Academy Award-winning actress John Crawford would help me do just that.

Chapter 14
Trog!

Our opponent following the Optimist game was First National Bank. They had only won a single game that season, so we expected another easy victory. Once again, we jumped to an early lead and never looked back. However, it was the game within the game that I will always remember. Ted was at the game. After we had taken a significant lead, Ted wanted to make the game more exciting. Trog, a movie about a scientist who discovers a primitive caveman, had just arrived at the theatres. The movie starred Joan Crawford in what would prove to be the last film of her remarkable career. The trailer to the movie looked awesome (well, at least to a 10-year-old kid). Ted promised me that he would take me to the movie if I struck out the side in the top of the third inning. That was all I needed to hear! When I took the mound, I was determined to throw smoke. When I struck out the first batter, I suspect my fist pump caught some off guard. The second strikeout simply fueled my intensity. When I struck out the third batter of the inning, my shout of excitement could have been interpreted as arrogance. I didn't care. I had a date to see Trog!

Imagine my disappointment when Ted informed me that my strikeout inning didn't count. "You didn't strike them out with nine straight strikes; therefore, it doesn't count." I was ready to kill him until he said he would give me a second chance.

Now called "immaculate innings," I completed mine during the next inning. The First National Bank batters didn't stand a chance. I threw nine consecutive strikes, with each subsequent pitch faster than the first. Nothing was going to stop me from seeing that movie. And when we did, I thought it was the most fantastic movie ever!

Some 20 years later, I watched Trog again, and this time, I would enjoy the cinematic experience with my young son, Travis. Unfortunately, over time, I guess either my memory had failed me, or my preferences for films had changed. All I know is that Trog had morphed into what was the worst movie ever made. What in the hell was I thinking? At least Travis didn't appear to mind; he fell asleep long before the exciting conclusion.

F.O. Day entered the All-Star break with 12 wins and two defeats. We were tied for first place with Optimist and Shakey's Pizza. We had defeated Shakey's rather handily earlier in the season, but their best player had missed the game due to strep throat. Shakey's had just beaten Optimist with him throwing a no-hitter.

Timmy and I were selected again to represent F.O. Day in the All-Star Game. We would also be teammates with the Shakey's pitcher. Our first introduction to him was not the most pleasant experience, but it would undoubtedly set the tone for meeting later in the season.

Chapter 15
All-Stars?

The annual All-Star Game was meant to be played by the very best players in the Rockville Boys Baseball Association. That is not what I experienced. Each All-Star team represented one of the two divisions within the league, and each team consisted of 20 players. During the course of the season not all teams played each other. For example, during the 1971 season, F.O. Day was not scheduled to play St. Mary's. We would only meet if we ended up facing each other in the playoffs. The All-Star Game allowed one to play with or against players you might not see during the regular season.

Timmy and I were the only players on our team whose father was not a coach. While some players were pretty good, it was clear that a few players were "All-Stars" in name only. They could thank their fathers for the privilege of being selected to the team.

We met the Shakey's Pizza pitcher at our first practice. His name was Bobby Puhl, and he took being arrogant to the next level. Typical baseball cleats at the time were your standard black ones. With the success of Joe Namath, some kids dared to wear white ones. Bobby chose neither. Instead, his cleats were spray-painted gold.

Bobby was boisterous and would brag to anyone who listened how great he was. His team only had two losses because he was out sick. He bragged that Shakey's would not lose another game all year. I could only hope we would meet again.

By the time of the All-Star Game, my left elbow and shoulder began to bother me more and more. Instead of resting my arm, Wayne continued to pitch me every game. I should have done a better job taking care of myself on days we didn't play. But I continued to play my fantasy baseball on the front steps of my parent's house.

My arm was killing me when our first All-Star practice began. I would rather have played first base or the outfield, but by that time, my reputation had preceded me. I was expected to pitch.

I can't say I tried my best during our three total practices. I saw no point in pitching in a meaningless game. I just went through the motions instead. I certainly was not throwing hard. As far as I was concerned, let Jimmy Brett or Bobby Puhl pitch.

I was on the bench as our team raced off to a sizeable lead. Jimmy started the game and threw well until Bobby replaced him at the top of the fourth. Bobby ran into immediate trouble, issuing a couple of walks, a hit batsman, followed by three consecutive singles. Our large lead had shrunk to 8-7.

I entered the game in the bottom of the inning pinch hitting for Timmy. I drew a two-out walk but was stranded at third following my second stolen base of the inning. Heading into the final frame, my coach told me to be prepared to pitch.

I started the top of the fifth in centerfield with Bobby still on the mound. His struggles continued as he walked three batters in a row. With the bases loaded and nobody out, the coach waved me in to pitch. As I stated, I did not want to pitch, and I especially did not want to bail Bobby out of the mess he created. Even worse, I did not have Andy to pitch to. To make things interesting, I went to a full count on the first two batters before striking them both out. The coaches and players shouted encouragement as the next batter came to the plate. All except Bobby, who was pouting on the end of the bench. The batter swung on the first pitch and popped the ball straight up. I made the catch to secure the victory. It was only then that I saw Wayne. He shook my hand to congratulate me before asking me who the kid with the gold cleats was.

Chapter 16
A Hot Summer

Our winning streak continued into August. My arm continued to bother me, but I kept quiet about it. It was a three-team race for first place, and nothing would drag me off the mound. We continued to win most of our games relatively comfortably until one hot afternoon when we faced Tippy's Taco House.

Tippy's players went to Meadow Hall Elementary and were unfamiliar to us. We would get to know their players once we attended junior high together. Tippy's was not among the best teams in the league, but they undoubtedly had some of the biggest players, a few of them were absolute monsters! Many of us just assumed that they had all flunked fifth grade. Multiple times.

The game was played on a hot and muggy afternoon. The temperature was in the 90s, and the humidity was awful. The game site was Welch Park, home of the Municipal Pool. The thought of swimming rather than playing baseball was certainly on our minds.

Perhaps it was the heat or lack of enthusiasm that caused the game to be a real struggle for us. Neither team could generate any offense. The temperature was so hot that Andy looked like a ripe tomato in his catching gear. I was convinced he was going to drop dead from heat stroke. Through four innings, we had only two base runners and no runs. Luckily, I was able to keep Tippy's scoreless as well.

I led off the top of the fifth inning. After fouling off several pitches, I eventually drew a walk. I immediately stole second base, then third base one pitch later. Sweat was pouring down my face as Timmy and then David went down swinging. As Andy advanced to the plate, I remained the go-ahead run in a scoreless game.

Coach Wayne called a timeout and met Andy halfway up the line. He whispered something in Andy's ear and returned to the third base coaching box. As he entered the box, he looked me in the eye and whispered, "Go on this pitch."

I broke for home just as the Tippy's pitcher toed the rubber. Halfway home, I prayed Wayne had just told Andy to take the pitch. Getting struck by a line drive ten feet from home plate was not my idea of fun.

The pitcher threw home, but I slid under the tag. The dirt was so hard that it felt like I was sliding on concrete. I felt my skin tear against the hard ground from my left armpit to my left knee. My painful steal of home put us in the lead, 1-0.

As I took the mound in the bottom of the fifth, the raspberry that resulted from my slide began to stick to my uniform. After each warmup pitch, I had to pull my jersey off my skin. And did I mention it was unbearably hot?

As fate would have it, I would face the heart of Tippy's lineup. Three players, all larger than Andy. Despite the heat, I felt strong. The adrenaline of having just stolen home was fueling me. I struck out the first batter on three pitches. The next batter never took the bat off his shoulder as I struck him out, too. The final batter looked almost afraid as he approached the plate. He never stood a chance. He took a called strike three to end the game.

It had been my best pitching performance of the year. A complete game one-hitter with 14 strikeouts. Continuing our team's season-long strategy, my aggressive baserunning gave us the only run we needed.

I went home and took a cold shower. Mom offered to spray my raspberry with Merthiolate, but I took a hard pass. Why did moms love that medicine anyway? Did they enjoy torturing their children? That shit stung like hell. Thank God it was eventually taken off the market by the FDA. Instead, I chugged water for the rest of the night. I felt like I had dropped 10 pounds off my already skinny frame. I fell asleep wondering if it would not be more fun to play a cold-weather sport like football or hockey.

Chapter 17
And Why Not Football?

My first exposure to organized football occurred a year earlier when I signed up for the Rockville Youth Instructional League. Practices were held every Saturday for eight weeks. Players were taught the basics of football, including how to block, tackle, and throw. Each player learned how to play every position. Following eight weeks of instruction, the league ended with an actual game between another instructional league team.

My best position was wide receiver. I was tall and fast and usually caught every pass thrown to me. Unfortunately, no one on my team could throw worth a damn, so I found myself blocking on most plays.

Halfway through the instructional course, I switched my position to outside linebacker. I enjoyed this position much more than wide receiver because I was involved in practically every play. I had a nose for the ball and enjoyed tackling my teammates.

Butch was home on leave for one of my practices, but he and Mom lasted less than five minutes watching from the sidelines. It was brutally cold with a steady wind. The temperature was well below freezing. I was all for canceling practice, but with one of our coaches wearing a tee shirt and shorts, the weather did not bother him. I suspect he was a complete idiot.

Our 90-minute practice could not end fast enough. I had long-lost feeling in my toes and just wanted to jump in a warm car. Tackling my teammates that morning on the frozen ground felt no different than tackling someone in the street. My hands and arms were scraped from the hard ground. When practice ended, it took ten minutes in the car for blood to finally flow from the scrapes. I had never been that cold in my life.

The day of our game finally arrived. Our opponent had enough players to field two teams. Their starting team consisted of players who looked considerably older than us and probably outweighed us by 20 pounds per player. We simply could not compete with the bigger kids. Only after taking a commanding lead, did their coach substitute players. We matched up much better when playing with kids our size. We lost 28-0. Perhaps I was just not suited to play football.

Nevertheless, I attempted organized tackle football once more when I was in junior high. The league was based on a player's weight. The minimum weight limit was 119 pounds, which happened to be my exact weight. I proved to be one of the smallest players in the league consistently getting my ass handed to me by much larger players.

My "official" football career ended on Thanksgiving Day

during my sophomore year of high school. Thanksgiving always meant our Turkey Bowl game played by my brothers and their friends. We would play the game on Thanksgiving morning and then go back home for a turkey feast.

Ted arrived late on this particular Turkey Bowl day, having had to work that morning at Flow. It was rainy and chilly, perfect weather for a game. When Ted arrived, he realized that he had left his cleats at home. Therefore, he demanded mine. I was used to being bullied. As the rain continued to fall, the field became a muddy quagmire. The footing was becoming treacherous, especially for one having had his cleats taken from him.

For three consecutive plays, I was open for passes but was either not seen or ignored by our quarterback. It was only after Ted told him that I was open that the next play was designed for me. Visions of catching the first touchdown of the game danced in my head. Instead, as the ball was snapped, I took one step and collapsed in the mud.

My left foot had become stuck in the mud as my momentum pushed me forward. I could feel something snap inside my knee. I grabbed my knee as I withered in the mud in agony. As Butch and Ted approached, both having been corpsmen like Dad, I expected they would help their kid brother. Instead, Ted simply said, "Get off the field, baby."

I made a 500-yard walk to the parking lot, my knee wobbling with each step. Butch's wife, Laurie, kindly drove me home. Dad was just finishing cooking the turkey. He took a look at my knee, shook his head, and proceeded to peel potatoes. Mom, however, seeing how badly swollen my knee was, drove me to the Bethesda Naval Hospital Emergency Room.

Dad's response was unsurprising. He had an incredible intolerance to pain. Seriously, who in their right mind would insist on never using novocaine when having cavities filled? He even expected our family pets to share his lack of pain. One day our dachshund, Fritz, sliced his belly on a piece of glass. Dad held Fritz down on his back while he stitched him up. Each time he would pull and tighten the suture, he would tell Fritz, "Don't you dare bite me."

Dad, without a doubt, inherited his intolerance to pain from his mom. Grandma Miller was one tough bird. She lived with my Uncle Paul. One day he came home from work to find her sitting in a chair with a bag of frozen vegetables resting on her foot. Her foot was swollen three times its normal size. Earlier that afternoon, she had stepped into a yellow jacket nest while picking berries. My uncle called her doctor to see what he should do. Her doctor said, "Well, is she breathing? If so, I guess she'll be fine." Grandma was 80 at the time.

Two years later, Grandma was diagnosed with breast cancer. The day after her double mastectomy, my Aunt Lois found her sitting in a chair in her hospital room, knitting a sweater. "Sign the damn papers, I wanna go home," she instructed her daughter.

Upon examination of my knee and subsequent X-rays, the doctor told me that my knee was dislocated. Upon draining fluid from the knee, I was placed in a straight cast and sent home. I had a feeling that his diagnosis was wrong.

When my cast was removed six weeks later, there was no pain when I walked. But if I walked for any extended distance, my knee would swell up like a balloon. Finally, after several weeks of this aggravation, an arthrogram was performed on my knee, and torn cartilage was detected.

I underwent surgery in the summer following my sophomore year. A surgery that was expected to last less than an hour took nearly four. The surgeon discovered the underbelly of my kneecap was utterly mush. Arthritis was already evident. He drilled into my leg bone, hoping calcium would form to protect the knee. During most of my surgery, Mom was in full panic mode in the waiting room. Having recently learned that Senator Ted Kennedy's son had his leg amputated due to cancer, Mom was convinced I was experiencing the same fate.

Well, I did not have cancer. But my knee was toast. I can thank Ted for crippling me. I would eventually have five more surgeries on my knee, including a total knee replacement in 2020. All because I was bullied into surrendering my cleats.

Playing any sport in high school was now out of the question. I could never pass the physical to be eligible to do so. When I tried to enlist in the Navy after graduating high school, my knee disqualified me from service. This would often prove a significant source of contention with Butch and Ted. "Why'd we have to serve, and you didn't?" It was then I would have to remind the two dummies that even if my knee was healthy, the United States was not at war in 1978.

My lone athletic event in high school occurred during my senior year. And to some students, it was the day that I became a legend.

Chapter 18
A Legend is Born

By my senior year, I was able to run again. I played softball the previous year with Butch and was finally able to play basketball with my friends. Each year, Richard Montgomery held a Faculty versus Student basketball game. I was asked to play in the game by my English teacher.

One of the game rules stipulated that the student team could only consist of two varsity players. This was not much help for us since our varsity basketball team was just as bad as our football and baseball teams. In fact, our only good team was our ping-pong squad, which consisted of several "boat people" who fled Vietnam. They were quite impressive. I never understood a damn thing they said, but they sure could smack the shit out of a ping-pong ball.

The Faculty team took the basketball matchup quite seriously. They even recruited the school custodian to play on their team. He was close to seven feet tall and, unbeknownst to us, had played professional basketball in Belgium. He was simply unstoppable.

The other good player for the Faculty was Mr. Lawrence, our Assistant Principal, an All-Conference player at a small school in Indiana. He was about 6'5", and during pregame warmups was throwing down dunks with ease. He was particularly hated by the stoners in our school because it seemed his sole focus was catching and punishing them for smoking pot in the bathroom and under the football bleachers.

The Faculty team jumped off to a big lead. I had yet to play and was becoming frustrated. The two varsity players were taking most of our shots, with very few of them finding the net.

I finally entered the game in the second quarter. A lazy pass was intercepted at midcourt by Mr. Lawrence. He had a clear path to his basket as I trailed behind him. As he went up for a dunk attempt, I got all ball as I swatted his shot from behind. Unfortunately, in doing so, my hand smacked him on the bridge of his nose as we both crashed to the floor. Blood poured out of his nose like a spiket as he turned aggressively toward me. I thought he was going to hit me before he regained his senses.

The stoners in the crowd gave me a standing ovation as the school nurse attended to Mr. Lawrence. I became their new best friend for the rest of the year. Even though I never hung out with their crowd, they would pat me on the back in the hallway and constantly offer me free joints.

I do not recall the final score of the basketball game. But it was pretty ugly. We were thoroughly abused. But by that time, I was used to being abused.

Chapter 19
I Have Not Eaten a Banana Since 1966

Having to surrender my cleats to Ted was nothing compared to other abuse I received from my other siblings. My sisters especially loved to torment me. Barb and Cathy are the reason I have not eaten a particular fruit in nearly 60 years.

My parents would buy groceries from the Navy Commissary. Feeding five kids meant buying food in large quantities. For example, they would buy 20 or more bananas rather than buying a few. Typically, my siblings and I would devour them within a few days. I can recall having sliced bananas with my morning cereal.

Occasionally, one banana would remain and turn brown as it began to spoil. Instead of throwing it away, it would remain on the kitchen table for all to see. Eventually, Dad would sit atop his throne and voice his displeasure, threatening never to purchase bananas again. Usually, his tirade would include the mentioning of starving kids in Africa and how we were fortunate not to live in such conditions. Unlike Ted, I never dared to say "Name one" like he did.

One of Dad's favorite expressions was, "Everything I say goes in one ear and out the other." One day, Ted decided to test this theory by sticking a finger in his ear and exclaiming, "No, it doesn't!" Dad immediately smacked him on his head. To this day, Ted is convinced his finger punctured his eardrum.

Other favorite Dad sayings:

- "Close the door! Were you born in a barn?"

- "You make a better door than a window." (When you were blocking his view of the TV)

- "I raised a bunch of goddamn idiots."

- "Can't you get that through your thick skull!" (While holding you in a headlock and pounding your skull with his knuckles)

- "You don't have the brains God gave a moron."

One day after Dad's most recent banana rant, Barb and Cath decided to ease his pain by making me eat the last banana. Cathy held me down as Barb shoved it into my mouth. Neither of them allowed me to escape until I had swallowed the remaining banana. Even now, I get queasy thinking about that rotten piece of fruit.

My abuse started at a very young age. I was 18 months old when my Mom accidentally (so she claimed) shut her bedroom door on my foot. She finally asked Cath to go see why I was crying. Cath screamed when she saw my baby toe hanging by a thread. Mom rushed me to Bethesda Naval Hospital to get stitches. While there, Mom was questioned for suspected child abuse because of the number of times my siblings had been seen there.

Since both Mom and Dad worked full-time, I spent my summers being watched over by my siblings. Typically, I could do whatever I wanted. Barb was more interested in finding her next boyfriend, and I would hang out with Cathy if I was not on the ball field or playing with my friends. But I was always subject to some sort of abuse.

One day, I made the mistake of revealing that I had a loose tooth. Barb decided to play dentist and told me she would remove the tooth herself. She made Cathy hold me down while she used a fishing line to wrap around the tooth. Barb then tied the other end of the line to the front door. Imagine my horror as I was subjected to Barb slamming the door several times before the tooth finally flung out of my mouth.

Playing ball or roughhousing was a regular occurrence within the Miller household despite our parents voicing their displeasure. Whether it was Butch tossing me a football, Ted bouncing a baseball against his bedroom wall, or boxing matches between siblings, indoor sports were the norm. Unfortunately, such fun and games often resulted in emotional distress to Mom and Dad.

Following the war, Dad received orders to report to a naval base in French Morocco. Since it was a two-year assignment, Mom, Butch, and infant Ted were allowed to come with him. My parents enjoyed their time in Morocco immensely. Mom especially loved the services of an elderly Moroccan woman named Isha to help with meals and household chores. Isha became incredibly close to three-year-old Ted, teaching him Arabic. Two years later, when my father was assigned duty in Birmingham, Alabama, Ted's kindergarten teacher struggled to rid his Arabic accent. Before too long, Ted's accent became part Arabic and part Alabamian. It is a wonder anyone could understand him.

While out to sea, Dad's ship had liberty in Brazil. There, he purchased several butterfly dishes. These colorful ceramic dishes consisted of dozens of beautiful butterfly wings in intricate patterns. When Dad returned to the States, my parents placed these dishes over the hallway, kitchen, and living room doors. I cannot imagine what these dishes would sell for today. Unfortunately, none of the Miller kids appreciated these dishes nor grasped the beauty they brought to each room. Frankly, they became nothing more than targets.

Whether it was from errant football throws, indoor frisbee

tosses, or batted nerf balls, these dishes never stood a chance. Sometimes, only a tiny piece of the dish would get damaged or only a tiny crack would appear. Dad would simply use Elmer's glue to repair it. Other times, dishes that hit the floor would explode in a cloud of dust. The butterfly wings inside would instantly vaporize.

The last dish was destroyed in 1967. Dad had already repaired the dish several times. Frankly, by that time, the dish had become an eyesore. But with it being the last one, Dad did what he could to keep the memory of the once beautiful dishes alive.

I am sorry that I was responsible for destroying the last dish. But seriously, what sane parent would buy a crossbow for their 7-year-old child for Christmas? I would have preferred their congratulations on my expert marksmanship.

I was not responsible for the other lost dishes. My older siblings destroyed them but blamed me. Being the youngest in the family also meant being falsely accused by others. My cries of innocence fell on deaf ears, and to persist only meant receiving the wrath of my siblings. Considering the number of times they falsely accused me, it is a wonder any of them thought I could be their ally? I was the first to point out a sibling's indiscretion whenever given the chance. Whether it was Barb sneaking a boyfriend into the basement or Cathy feeding the family dog a portion of that night's mystery meal, I would rat them out in a heartbeat.

The day that Ted and Barb nearly scalded me was one I will never forget. Mom and Dad were out, when chaos erupted in the living room. Ted was playing dodgeball with Cathy as Barb was in the kitchen making butterscotch pudding. An errant throw struck the handle of the pot on the stove just as I was walking into the kitchen. The pot filled with steaming pudding flew up into the air and landed on my back. I quickly removed my tee shirt to avoid third-degree burns, however, my back looked like I had spent a week at the beach without sunscreen.

Sensing that he could have hurt me badly, Ted transformed into my new best friend. In return for not ratting him out to our parents, he allowed me to hang out with his friends that day. Heck, he even bought me lunch! His efforts to buy my silence lasted until my parents got home. The front door had not even closed before I informed them that Ted had tried to kill me.

My abuse was not limited to just my siblings. At an early age, Mom did her best to torment me as well. She was Cathy's Brownies troop leader, and one day they were guests on the Bozo the Clown Show. Mom thought it was a good idea that her toddler son come to the show too.

During a television break, Bozo, portrayed by the late Willard Scott, mingled with the audience. When he attempted to pick me up, I freaked out. Seriously, what 18-month-old baby wants anything to do with a grown man wearing clown makeup and a big red nose? I became so hysterical that Mom was asked to remove me from the studio. To this day, I still do not like clowns.

A few years later, Mom thought buying her kids boxing gloves was a good idea. One day Cathy and I were sparring when she punched me so hard that I fell back into our living room bookcase. My eye missed the edge of the bookcase by mere millimeters. Only by sheer luck did I not lose it. A life of wearing an eye patch was that close to becoming a reality. By the following day, my eye was a bit puffy, and I convinced Mom that I needed to stay home from school. Cathy was stunned with her decision, and over 50 years later still bitches about it.

Amazingly, I survived childhood.

Chapter 20
A Slaughter Well Deserved

Our next game was against a team sponsored by WINX, a radio station located in downtown Rockville. The WINX head coach was a crusty old man who seemed more interested in taunting his opponents than coaching his own team. Even before the game began, an air of tension-filled the air.

Our games started with the respective managers exchanging lineup cards and listening to the ground rules from the umpire. Things got off to a rough start when the WINX manager refused to shake Wayne's hand. That was just the start of what was to come.

We were the home team, so I took the mound to begin my warmup tosses. After throwing a couple of pitches, I heard the WINX manager tell his players, "Look at the size of their catcher! He must spend his day eating candy and ice cream." He was making fun of Andy's weight. I called Andy to the mound to tell him to ignore the manager, but I could tell he was upset and mad. Andy would let out his frustration later in the game.

The WINX team was not very good, so I was not sure what their manager was trying to prove. Perhaps he was just an asshole, but his taunts continued throughout the game. When he saw David and his long hair, he cried out, "I thought girls aren't allowed in this league."

I held WINX scoreless in the top of the first. As we entered our dugout, Wayne instructed us to ignore the WINX manager. "Shut him up using your bats," he suggested. Well, we took his advice and pounded WINX unmercifully. At the end of two innings, we led 21-0. And we were not finished.

It was bad enough that the WINX manager was taunting kids, but then he focused his wrath on Wayne. After calling him a "hippie" and "long-haired freak," some fans in the stands started laughing. I became upset when I saw Mrs Richardson was among those who were laughing.

To Wayne's credit, he ignored these outbursts, but his team did not. We were ready to score as many runs as possible. We became an angry team, and the focus of our rage was the WINX manager.

Andy drove a double over the center fielder's head late in the game. Timmy followed with a single to left. Ignoring Wayne's hold sign at third, Andy barreled for home. The throw beat Andy by a good 10 feet, but he had no intention of sliding. Instead, he crashed into the catcher. I was the on-deck hitter, and I have never forgotten the look on the umpire's face. His mouth was agape, no doubt believing he had just witnessed a murder. The catcher's mask, glove, and ball flew to the backstop as he crumpled to the ground. I was amazed that he eventually rose to his feet. Meanwhile, Andy turned to the WINX manager and said, "I think I'll have my Hershey bar now."

The final score was 39-0. Our only regret was that we did not score more runs. My lasting memory of the game was pitching to a WINX batter who was certainly the shortest player in the league. Rather than try to hit the ball, the WINX manager instructed him to crouch at the plate, his butt nearly touching the ground. I guess that was his way to try to draw walks, but it did not bother me a bit. I struck him out each time he came to bat. What was his coach trying to accomplish? How could a player ever improve if he never swung a bat? His coach was both obnoxious, as well as a poor teacher and coach.

Teaching. That was something that I had dreamed of doing. Years later, my dreams came true.

Chapter 21
Donald Duck

All Twinbrook Elementary fifth graders participated in Career Week. Students were asked to choose career paths that interested them and study the nuances of each job. My three top choices were a professional baseball player, a career in the Navy, and a school teacher. Little did I know that at age 10, two of my choices would be eliminated due to sports injuries.

I earned my associate's degree at Montgomery College and later enrolled at the University of Maryland. Since I often worked two jobs, I only took one or two classes each semester. My final two classes at Maryland were math courses. While I always got decent grades in math in high school, it was never my favorite class.

The first math class at Maryland was just a basic college introductory course. When I read the course catalog, I noticed the class was being offered as both a three and four-credit course. The difference between the two classes was that the four-credit one was intended for students with a "math phobia." Each week, a psychologist would meet with the class to deal with their anxiety issues. That course was for me! I figured I would be surrounded by students who disliked math just like me.

Unfortunately, the day before this class was scheduled to begin, I was notified that it had been canceled. Not enough students had enrolled in it. I was automatically enrolled in the three-credit class instead.

I was nervous when I attended my first class, but I soon found out the course was extremely easy. I often finished quizzes and tests in a matter of minutes. One night, while on a break, the professor told me that I was doing very well in her class. I replied that I thought her math class had to be the easiest class that the University of Maryland offered. She smiled and shook her head. She said the easiest class was one not found in the course catalog. It was the math class that most of the Maryland athletes enrolled in. If that was the case, I am amazed that any athlete could flunk out of school.

My last class was Statistics 100. After the first night, I was walking to my car, wondering how many times I would need to repeat the class just to earn a D. After all, a D meant a diploma! I found the class to be extremely difficult, but I got through it. I just question the sanity of anyone who enrolls in multiple courses in statistics.

I would eventually enroll at Johns Hopkins University to obtain a Masters in Education. After a long career in security, I was ready to pursue my dream of becoming a school teacher. While enrolled at Hopkins, I began substitute teaching in Montgomery

County, Maryland, and I absolutely loved it! I primarily subbed from kindergarten through the fifth grade. Having coached teenagers, I had no interest in teaching them as well.

During training to become a substitute, our instructor advised us to use any special talents one might possess to make the substitute teaching process more enjoyable. One of my talents is talking like Donald Duck. I would inform my students that if they did their work, Donald Duck might give them high fives. That might sound silly, but it works! It is amazing how talking like a duck kept my students focused on their work.

I only taught junior high a few times, and let me tell you, junior high teachers do not get paid enough money! A neighbor asked me to sub at her daughter's junior high. Her daughter was the school cafeteria manager and she promised to feed me real good. Well, not one to turn down a good meal, I accepted a substitute teaching position at her school.

I was scheduled to sub for an eighth-grade history class. The teacher was a young guy right out of college who had to attend training that day. I met him in his class before his departure, and he provided me with his lesson plans.

The teacher told me that his first couple of classes consisted of pretty good kids, but to keep an eye on his fifth-period class. "They can be a bit rowdy after lunch," he explained. Well, the first four classes were a breeze. I began to think the students were the offspring of the Stepford Wives because their behavior was picture-perfect

Things changed after the arrival of the fifth-period class. Several of the students were quite rambunctious. I was having difficulty getting them to settle down when one of them asked, "Mr. Miller, what do you do when you're not subbing?" The student had just provided me with the opening I needed! My answer caught their attention when I replied that I was a prison guard. One student asked if I carried weapons in the cellblock. I replied, "We are not allowed to carry weapons in prison, but I recently had to break a prisoner's leg."

You could have heard a pin drop as the students contemplated my response. One student said, "Did you use a billy club to break his leg?" I said a billy club was considered a weapon, so a guard does not carry one. "Well, how did you break his leg?" another student asked. "With my bare hands," came my response. The entire classroom sat stunned.

For the remainder of the period, I answered prison questions. Since my only prison experience came from watching Cool Hand Luke, The Green Mile, and the Shawshenk Redemption, I tried my best to make my answers sound legitimate. Heaven knows what they told their parents when they got home.

The final class of the day proved to be my most challenging. Within a few minutes, I had to break up fights between four students. For the only time in my substitute teaching career, I had to push the security button found in each classroom. And, of course, the one time I did the button failed to work. Instead of teaching the class, I spent the entire period keeping the four students separated.

I survived the final class and was in the middle of writing my notes to the teacher when he returned from training. He told me he should have warned me about the last-period class. Gee, you think? The look on his face was one of utter defeat. "I suffer every day waiting for that class to end," he said.

I never had the opportunity to teach his class again. His name never appeared on a substitute vacancies listing. I suspect his teaching career did not last long. As for me, my junior high substitute teaching days were over.

Chapter 22
I Nearly Killed Wayne.
Again.

Entering the final week of the regular season, we remained tied with Optimist and Shakey's Pizza for first place in our division. St. Mary's had long wrapped up their division title and awaited the winner of our division to begin the City Championship series.

Our next-to-last opponent in the regular season was Peoples Drug Store. They had only won a handful of games, but after our close call with Tippy's Taco House, we were not taking anyone lightly. While we ended up winning the game relatively comfortably, I nearly killed Wayne for the second time in a year.

The first time occurred the previous season at Dogwood Park. I was pitching, which meant the game was already out of hand. Wayne was leaning over the railing of our dugout just as the batter lined a foul ball straight at him. Unable to react in time, the ball struck him squarely on his head as he fell to the ground.

I was convinced that my pitched ball had just killed my coach.

Everyone on the team was aware of the steel plate in his head. No one knew if he would get back up when he went down. Thankfully, Wayne never lost consciousness, and when he was finally back on his feet, he was prepared to continue coaching the game. Dad put that idea to bed. He dragged Wayne to his car and drove him to Bethesda Naval Hospital. Dad knew that even a slight movement of the steel plate could have tragic consequences. Following a negative CAT scan, Wayne was released by the doctor.

The following season, the same thing nearly happened again. Once again, I was on the mound, and a foul ball was launched toward our dugout with Wayne as its intended target. Thankfully, the ball only struck the bill of Wayne's cap. He was lucky. We all hoped that luck would stay with us as our season drew to a close.

Chapter 23
Cathy

Lucky is not how I would describe my sister. Who knew that Cat Scratch Fever was an actual disease, and just not a Ted Nugent song? Cathy can attest that it is indeed a real illness which caused her to miss several weeks of school while in the seventh grade. Later in life, after seeking medical treatment for a bunion on the bottom of her foot, her foot became severely infected, resulting in the amputation of two of her toes (hence her nickname "The Sloth"). On the bright side, it is easy to track her footsteps on a beach. Cathy's biggest problem is her total trust in her doctors. It was only after her podiatrist recommended the amputation of her foot that she finally sought a second opinion.

Cathy broke her thumb a few years ago after falling in the snow. Surgery was performed to have pins inserted into her thumb for stability. I drove her to her appointment weeks later when she had the pins removed. Following the procedure, we drove to Norfolk to visit my grandchildren. Within an hour, Cathy began to complain of pain in her hand. I offered to turn around, but she assured me that she would be fine.

By the following morning, it was clear that she was not fine. Her temperature had risen to over 104 degrees during the night.

She notified her doctor, who instructed her to return to the hospital. Cathy looked terrible. She was nauseous as the pain in her hand increased. As we drove back to Maryland, I was convinced she would die in my car. Upon our arrival at the hospital, she immediately underwent surgery to clean out the infection in her hand. This would prove to be the first of many such surgeries.

Over time, Cathy's hand began to atrophy. Three of her fingers became bent, and she was unable to straighten them out. Surgeries were performed to kill the nerves in her hand. Still, her fingers remained frozen. Cathy was in constant pain. She finally suspected that she had chosen the wrong surgeon after he performed a tenth surgery on her hand and informed her that he was moving to California.

Cathy found her next doctor at Johns Hopkins. Upon her initial consultation with him, I suggested that perhaps it would be easier for him to simply amputate her hand. After all, Cathy was left-handed. Did she really need her right hand? The doctor looked at me like I was demented. Several surgeries later, I again kiddingly suggested amputation. Imagine my surprise when he said he still had one or two ideas before amputation would be considered.

Cathy still has her right hand, though her hand resembles a claw. She still enjoys a happy life even though she is in constant pain. Her favorite pastime is visiting casinos to play slots. Her clawed hand has proven to be no problem whatsoever. It perfectly fits the slot machine lever.

Cathy was often the butt of jokes while growing up. Since she was the only blonde in our family this led to many questions for Mom as to what exactly she was doing when Dad was away at sea. Butch and Ted remember her being very friendly with the mailman, but Mom never admitted to any indiscretions. Instead, we all just teased Cathy that she was adopted.

Upon my graduation from high school, I went to work with other family members at Flow. Cathy was my first boss. We worked in a repository that provided tissue typing trays used for kidney transplants, bone marrow transplants, and paternity testing. It was here in the repository I first met Lawrence McBrien, aka Larry McBrain, aka Larry McBoob, aka Larry McBomb. Cathy had already started writing a book about him. Entitled "Larry's Song," it was a historical record of every dumb thing he did or said since he worked at Flow. I became the book's new editor. Larry was going to be the central character in my Pulitzer Prize-winning book. Visions of John Candy portraying him in a movie danced in my head. I was going to be rich and famous. But I will talk about McBoob later.

Chapter 24
Barb

I was not as close to Barb as I was to Cathy. Being several years older than me, Barb preferred the company of her friends. Except for her playing dentist with my tooth, helping to shove a rotten banana down my throat and nearly scalding me with hot butterscotch pudding, we rarely hung out together.

I can still recall the time that Barb had three different boyfriends at my parent's house at the same time. Her old beau was a friend of Ted's, and he happened to stop by the house just as Barb's current boyfriend was there. He was a private in the United States Army who had dated her for a couple of months. He had come to the house as a surprise while on a 48-hour pass from Fort Dix. No one was more surprised than my sister. The third boyfriend turned out to be Bill, my future brother-in-law. He and Barb had just started dating, and I guess Barb had forgotten to tell the Army guy.

Each boyfriend sat in a corner of the living room, staring at each other. Dad was nervously pacing in the front yard, smoking one Lucky Strike cigarette after another. Meanwhile, Barb pleaded with Mom for help. Mom was having none of that and informed Barb that she was on her own.

One of the highlights of summer was buying ice cream off the Good Humor truck. Neighborhood kids would converge on the truck after hearing its bells announce its arrival. The Good Humor man was a mean old guy who would yell at kids if they took too long to place their order. If you didn't have exact change, he would shoot daggers at you. Except for Barb. She was the only person he gave free ice cream to. Why was she so special? I guess some things are best left untold.

Barb would later become trained in medical transcriptions. One of her first jobs was working as a transcriber at Leland Memorial Hospital in Riverdale Park, Maryland. Her office was located near the emergency room. Barb took pleasure in telling us all of the weird things she experienced, often in gory detail. From the man who waddled in with a lightbulb stuck in his rectum to the man carrying severed fingers in a paper bag as a result of a lawnmower accident, Barb always had interesting and bizarre stories to tell.

Unlike Cathy, Barb enjoyed drinking alcohol. This would almost cause Dad to have a heart attack. Dad was never a drinker. On the rare occasion, he would share a beer with Mom. But it was whiskey, specifically Wild Turkey, which caused Dad's blood pressure to rise.

For several years, Wild Turkey would issue porcelain decanters that depicted magnificently molded wildlife. From turkeys and eagles to bears and foxes, these decanters were adored by my nature-loving father. He displayed the decanters throughout the house, never opening a decanter that was filled with whiskey.

One night, Barb decided to open a decanter to make drinks for her friends. Over the course of the next several months, more decanters were opened. After emptying each decanter, she would replace it on the shelf without Dad knowing that the decanters were empty.

Finally, one night, while playing canasta, Dad took a decanter from a shelf to show his brother who was visiting from Pennsylvania. It was only then that Dad discovered what Barb had done. He was devastated. Despite having no interest whatsoever in consuming the whiskey himself, Dad was still upset that Barb had "ruined" his whiskey collection.

Family canasta night had long been a Miller tradition. Typically divided into men's versus women's teams, canasta was a way for family members to bash each other. And believe me, nothing was deemed off-limits. Whether it was making fun of relatives or questioning which grandchild was most likely to end up in prison, canasta was often the source of dark humor fun.

Mom enjoyed a beer or two, but during canasta nights, Barb could always be counted upon to provide Mom with mixed drinks. And when Mom finally began to slur her words, it was time to bring a tape recorder to the kitchen table. That is when the real nasty insults would commence. If I had a dollar for every time Mom said, "We need to erase this tape," I would have retired a rich man.

During one particular canasta night, Barb stunned my parents when she asked them if they still had sexual intercourse. This led Dad to shake his head in utter disgust while lighting another cigarette, while Mom looked at Barb, unable to say a word.

Barb had always wanted to own a Saint Bernard. So for Christmas one year, I bought her one. Knowing that her husband, Bill, would probably not be happy with the addition of a puppy to their apartment, I bought him a large rat snake. Bill always loved snakes, and I figured that if Barb got a pet for Christmas, so should he.

The snake was supposed to have been fed one live mouse a week. Before visiting my parents house, Bill dropped a mouse into the snake aquarium and left the apartment. A snowstorm left them stranded at my parents' house for a few days. Upon their arrival back to their apartment, they noticed blood smeared all over the aquarium glass. As Bill approached the aquarium, the live mouse appeared out of a hole in the dead snake. Evidently, the snake had tried to eat the mouse live, and the mouse had literally eaten itself out of the snake's stomach. Barb compared the aquarium to a murder scene and ordered Bill to flush the mouse down the toilet. Bill did not have the heart to do so. He considered the mouse a gladiator and thought it had earned its freedom. Bill released the mouse into the woods instead.

Chapter 25
Jesus, He Shot Me!

Our last regular season game was against Hot Shoppes, and once again, we struggled to score runs. A victory would leave us in a tie for first place. A defeat would likely eliminate us from playoff contention.

After discovering I had left my pitcher's glove at home, I started the game on the wrong foot. I threw my warmup pitches wearing my first base mitt. The Hot Shoppes' coach complained to the umpire that wearing the first base mitt gave me an unfair advantage in fielding balls hit to me. The opposing coach complained even more when I fielded a ground ball in the first inning.

The umpire decided that I would use a borrowed mitt from one of the players on the other team. We would share the mitt each inning. This only seemed to aggravate the other coach even more. We entered the last inning tied 2-2. Using the borrowed mitt had not bothered me in the least and I completely ignored the complaining from the Hot Shoppes dugout.

I led off our half of the inning with a single to right. I stole second base to put us a hit away from victory. Timmy lined a single off the glove of the shortstop. Making sure that the ball was not caught, I got a delayed jump off the bag. Wayne was waving me home as I reached third base, and I slid into home with the winning run. As I was just getting to my feet to join our victory celebration, I felt a hard thump to my chest. I collapsed back onto the ground, unable to breathe. My first thought was that our opponent's coach had just shot me. I guess using my first base mitt had indeed pissed him off. Thankfully, my collapse was not the result of a bullet but an arrant throw from the outfielder.

The victory kept us in first place. We would have to await the game results for Optimist and Shakey's Pizza to determine if they remained tied with us. Nevertheless, the playoffs were looming, and Wayne soon proved to be our good luck charm.

Chapter 26
Tails Always Win!

We received word that Optimist and Shakey's Pizza had both won their final regular season games, resulting in a three-way tie for first in our division. None of us held the tiebreaker. We lost to Optimist and defeated Shakey's. Optimist had beaten us but lost to Shakey's. Shakey's had defeated Optimist but lost to us. A sudden-death playoff format would be used to determine the division winner.

The three coaches met at a local bar to participate in a coin toss. The odd team out would receive a first-round bye. Wayne called tails as all three coaches flipped a coin at the same time. When only one coin landed tails, F.O. Day was awarded the bye. Wayne then proceeded to have his own celebration by ordering a couple of drinks. The other coaches refused to join him.

Optimist and Shakey's Pizza squared off on the following Saturday. Wayne suggested that we all attend the game to scout our playoff opponent. The game featured two of the best pitchers in the league and was scoreless after two innings. Both Jimmy Brett and his spray-painted cleated rival, Bobby Puhl, were throwing well. Whatever nerves Bobby exhibited during the All-Star Game was gone.

Revenge was certainly on our minds. We all wanted another shot at Optimist. This time I would not have to worry about exceeding my innings pitch limit. If not Optimist, I relished the opportunity to pitch against Puhl.

For fifth-grade boys, watching and playing a game are two different things. After watching a couple of innings, we all grew bored. Andy had brought his football, and soon we found ourselves in a game of tackle. It was about an hour later that Wayne informed us that Shakey's had scored the winning run in their last at-bats. We went back to playing now knowing who our opponent was going to be. I wondered if Bobby was planning a fresh coat of paint for his cleats. I was just happy to be facing him. I had not forgotten the arrogance he displayed during our All-Star practices. Here was my opportunity to shut him up once and for all.

Chapter 27
In Over Our Heads

I promised to tell you another football story, so here it is. When I worked at Flow, my brothers and I played for two years in the Rockville Men's Touch Football League. And to put it bluntly, we truly sucked. Our overall record was 1 win and 19 defeats. And our sole victory was by forfeit!

Before you laugh too much, our forfeit triumph comes with a disclaimer. We were awarded the victory after our opponents could not field their seven-man squad. The other team's tardy player arrived after the referees left the field. We proceeded to play a scrimmage game which we won. So, I would prefer that the forfeit simply be ignored.

Sponsored by Flow, our team typically started the season with 14 players. Seven players would play offense, and seven would play defense. Despite being the best quarterback on the team, Butch preferred to play defense. Therefore, I joined him and Ted on defense playing cornerback.

The playing field was measured every 20 yards using traffic cones. Downs and distances were determined where the ball was placed in relation to the cones. Therefore, plays could start as far away as first and twenty or as close as first and one. We typically did not have to worry about first downs because our team generated little offense. Our line could not block worth a damn and our quarterback could barely throw more than ten yards.

We were trailing one game late by the score of 28-0. We faced a fourth and five near midfield. I was our punter and was instructed by our head coach to punt it away. I thought kicking the ball trailing by four touchdowns was a dumb thing to do, so instead, I whispered to Butch to go out for a pass, and I would throw it to him. Our fake punt was a success, and our coach was so thrilled that he appointed me our new quarterback.

Knowing I could not throw a football worth a damn but knowing Butch could, I called our next play. I was to take the snap and roll to my right. When the defense pursued me, I would throw a cross-field lateral to Butch, who in turn would throw a long pass to Ted.

The timing of the play sputtered from the start. The ball was snapped over my head several yards behind me. Since it was a live ball, I quickly retreated and fell on it. Two defensive linemen ran right past me but failed to touch me. At this point, Butch screamed that he was open, so I lateraled the ball to him from my knees. Butch threw a perfect pass from beyond midfield to the back of the end zone, a pass of over 60 yards. One of our teammates, Willie Jones, was running near the end line. The pass hit Willie directly on the side of his face, and he crumpled to the ground. He looked like he had just been shot from the top of a school book depository.

Willie returned to our huddle, still trying to shake the cobwebs from his brain. He turned to Butch and said, "Hey, you need to tell me if you are throwing to me."

By the time the season ended, half of our team had quit. That meant the rest of us could now play the entire game. And that made the games more enjoyable. We didn't win any more games, but with Butch finally agreeing to play quarterback, we at least started scoring touchdowns.

I have never let Butch forget about one game we played. At the half, we were winning 7-0. I had several receptions, including a touchdown and the extra point conversion. But in the second half, I was not targeted once. Despite often waving my arms frantically, Butch refused to throw me the ball. After subsequently losing the game 12-7, I asked Butch why he had ignored me. He replied that some of our teammates were upset with him for throwing so many passes to me in the first half, so he just stopped throwing to me. Butch was more concerned about the hurt feelings of his teammates than playing to win the game. Is it any wonder why we sucked?

Chapter 28
Yep, I was Obnoxious

The division championship game against Shakey's Pizza was played on a Saturday afternoon at Monument Park. The park sat in a ravine surrounded by steep hills. Parents and fans from both teams spread out blankets to watch the game.

For the first time in days, my arm was not bothering me. The pain in my elbow had subsided and I threw well during warmups. In the meantime, Bobby Puhl, wearing his gold cleats, was doing the same next to his dugout.

A coin flip determined home field, and Wayne was called upon to call the toss. Once again, he called tails, and once again, his choice proved correct. We would be the home team, and I would take the mound first. It was just a matter of time before tempers began to flare.

Bobby was Shakey's leadoff hitter. As he settled into the batter's box, Andy quietly inquired about his gold-sprayed cleats. Specifically, Andy asked him, "Are those the same shoes you wear to dance class?" Bobby dropped his bat and offered a few choice words about Andy's Mom. Fortunately, the umpire got between them before punches were thrown, and then warned both teams that further incidents would result in player ejections.

Bobby was still upset as I threw my first pitch, a called strike right down the middle. My next pitch was a fastball on the outside corner, which Bobby took again for strike two. He immediately turned to the umpire to argue the call. After just two pitches, Bobby was proving to be a headcase. He was someone I thought I could mess with. Boy, was I right.

I blew strike three right past him. He belatedly swung when the ball was already in Andy's mitt. Bobby slammed his bat to the ground and glanced at me as he walked to his dugout. I doubt he appreciated my smile back to him. I surrendered a two-out single but escaped the inning with the game scoreless. Like my pitching counterpart, I would bat leadoff. And I intended to enjoy myself.

As Bobby completed his warm-up tosses, he still looked pretty pissed. I suspect him watching Andy practicing ballet moves in our dugout did not help matters. As he went into his windup to deliver his first pitch, I called timeout and stepped out of the batter's box. I pretended that a gnat had flown into my eye. Bobby was not buying my charade and yelled for me to step back into the box.

Since it worked once, why not do it again? So when Bobby went into his windup, I again stepped out of the box. But this time, I was warned by the umpire to stop my antics. But my mission was accomplished, Bobby was so angry that it became easy to get inside his head.

Bobby's first two pitches to me bounced to the backstop. His coaches yelled for him to calm down as I grounded his third pitch up the middle for a single. I took a long lead off first base daring him to throw over. And when he did, I quickly dived back. I laughed as the first baseman threw the ball back to him. A second pickoff attempt was also unsuccessful, and Bobby was about to stroke out when I continued to laugh at him.

I stole second base and then scored our first run on a single to left by David. Timmy and Andy then hit back-to-back home runs, and our lead ballooned to 4-0. I retired Shakey's in order in the top of the second and third and felt confident that the game was ours. But first, I had to mess with Bobby just a little bit more.

I came to bat in the bottom of the third with the bases loaded. By this time, our lead had stretched to 6-0, and Bobby was struggling. Our bench was riding him pretty hard, and he seemed more interested in returning our taunts than concentrating on batters. On his first pitch to me, I lined a triple to right field. Only the ball rolling out of play prevented me from my first grand slam since I had played softball.

Standing on third base, I began taunting Bobby once again. I dived back safely following three consecutive pickoff attempts.

After each attempt, I laughed and told him that his attempts were not even close.

Ted was sitting on the hill above the third base bag and heard the banter between Bobby and me. I don't doubt that Ted was among those fans who laughed when I was finally picked off third, when the third baseman blocked the base path as I attempted to dive back. Interference should have been called, but I guess the umpire had grown tired of my mouth as well.

As I walked off the field following the pickoff, a Shakey's fan cried out, "Thank God they finally shut that asshole up!" Ted would later say that I deserved it. "You were obnoxious. You were lucky somebody didn't beat your ass."

Two innings later, we finished the game with a 9-0 victory. I finished with a one-hitter with 12 strikeouts. We could not congratulate Bobby on a successful season because he refused to shake our hands following the game. Instead, he flipped us the bird while walking to his parent's car. Up next was St. Mary's and the best of three championship series. It would prove to be a very tough series. Not the "war" that many professional athletes call their games, but one that proved physically and emotionally draining to me. Besides, it would be several years before I experienced "war."

Chapter 29
Combat Sports

Once I flunked my physical with the Navy during my senior year of high school, I figured I would never have to experience war like Dad, Wayne, or his Marine Corps friends. The closest thing to war would occur a few years later when I worked at Flow. We had heard about a new business operating in the woods of Northern Virginia called The Survival Game. Players were divided into two teams, each player was provided a paint gun, and a new form of Capture the Flag was played. Several of my coworkers reserved a date to play.

Our games were scheduled for a Saturday morning at 8 a.m. The temperature was already in the 80s and rising. The humidity caused sweat to pour off your arms. My team included Cathy, Ted, my brother-in-law Bill, and several of my softball teammates.

The biggest mistake many of us had made was staying up late the night before. We played basketball at a local park and went to a bar afterward for some refreshments. By the time the paintball game began, I was convinced I was sweating alcohol from my pores.

The object of the game was to find the home base of your

opponent, capture their flag, and return it to your base without getting shot. Games would start and end with the judge's whistle.

Within seconds of the start of our game, we became hopelessly lost in the woods. We finally came across a path and followed it deeper into the woods. We walked in a single-file line with me trailing the pack. I was certainly feeling the effects of staying out late the night before.

After a few minutes, Bill returned to the rest of us. He told us that he had discovered our opponent's base and their flag. We all encouraged Bill to attack the base. Within seconds of grabbing the flag, Bill was shot several times in the back. He passed the flag to Cathy, and she too was shot. Panic set in after she handed the flag to me. I began running as shots rang out all around me. I outraced the other team but got lost in the process. I eventually stumbled across my home base despite having to avoid getting shot by my own players.

We would play this game several times over the next year. I was eventually hired to be a judge for the game. I spent every weekend for the next several months watching people shoot each other with paintballs.

I left Flow to work for the American Red Cross. It was not long before several Red Cross employees expressed an interest in playing paintball games. We soon challenged Flow to a match.

They certainly took our challenge seriously. With our games scheduled three weeks in advance, Flow began sending us daily letters informing us that we were in trouble, that they were prepared to massacre us.

One example of their attempt to intimidate us occurred after a Flow Laboratory technician sliced his hand on a broken glass test tube. While the wound required stitches, the tech was first required to bleed on several pages of Flow stationery before his trip to the hospital. These pages, copiously splattered with his dried blood, were subsequently used to send us more taunting letters.

Flow's biggest attempt at psychological warfare occurred on the day before our battle. A six foot funeral wreath was delivered to our building. I have no idea what this wreath cost, but unbeknownst to Flow, their attempts to scare us failed miserably.

In actuality, our team only consisted of a few Red Cross employees. The remaining players on our team were "mercenaries" I had enlisted from games that I had officiated over the past several months. These players were die-hard paintball players. Most played weekly. Some played both Saturdays and Sundays. Flow would not know what hit them.

I supplied our players with Red Cross flags to attach to their cars to display when they arrived at the game site. But my ruse proved ineffective when Flow players observed that most of my players came equipped with their own personal paintball guns, military surplus clothing, and equipment.

To say that our games were lopsided would be an understatement. Flow stood no chance. My group of mercenaries wiped them from the field in record times. None of the games we played were competitive. I took great pleasure shooting both Butch and Ted during the course of the action. My lone regret was not shooting Cathy too. But she would get her comeuppance.

Throughout the morning's games, Flow players were being eliminated left and right. All except Cath. Somehow, despite wearing a bright tee shirt and shorts and not camouflage like her teammates, Cath avoided being struck by paintballs.

During breaks between each game, Cath began to flaunt her success. She openly bragged about being the lone Flow player who had yet to be shot. Finally, after the last game of the morning, Cath began to brag once more again. At that point, her teammate, Butch, had heard enough. He pointed his paint gun mere inches from her leg and shot her in the thigh. For weeks afterwards her leg bruised an array of colors.

One day, my Red Cross boss approached me with a business idea. Why couldn't we start our own paintball business? With weekend games generating up to $15,000 in business, the idea was very intriguing.

My boss and I, along with two others, contributed $2,500 each to start our company. We purchased 100 paint guns along with sufficient amounts of paintballs and CO_2 cartridges. We rented a large tract of land near the Manassas National Battlefield. We named our business Combat Sports.

At our grand opening, over 100 players attended. I was taking a break in our storage trailer when a Virginia State Trooper pulled into our parking lot. He inquired, "What in the hell is going on here?" He was not impressed when I described the rules of the game. He then asked, "Let me see your permits." Oh oh.

To say that we made business mistakes was an understatement. Our lawyer informed us that permits were not necessary. I never did learn where he earned his law degree, but his advice was all wrong. We had to appear before the Prince William County Board of Supervisors in order to obtain these permits.

Many of our players showed up at the hearing to offer their support. Many were given opportunities to speak to the Supervisors directly. My favorite speaker was a first-grade teacher who had played the game several times. Unfortunately, you could barely hear her say a word. She could have played the role of The Low Talker on Seinfeld. Her testimony proved worthless.

Ultimately, our biggest mistake was renting land directly across from an orphanage. We thought that the director of the orphanage had no problems with us being in his neighborhood. We were wrong. His lawyer stood before the Supervisors and claimed we were warmongers intent on harming children. And when he pleaded for the children's lives, I knew we were finished. The Supervisors voted against us. Combat Sports was out of business.

I would have to find other ways to get rich. Maybe that Pulitzer Prize award-winning book about McBoob was the way to go.

Chapter 30
Championship Series
Game 1

None of us realized just how good St. Mary's was until we squared off in game one. Their roster only consisted of ten players, and all proved to be good players. There was not an easy out in their lineup.

As I mentioned previously, St. Mary's was the only team in the Rockville Boys Baseball Association that was not subject to the draft lottery. Perhaps it was because they were the only private school in the league, or perhaps since their school was smaller than others, only ten of their students signed up to play. I call bullshit on both of those suggestions. Was it just plain coincidence that every player in their lineup was good?

There was no doubt in my mind that Twinbrook Elementary would have been virtually unbeatable if the team consisted of its ten best players. Optimist was always loaded with talent and F.O. Day had proven we could compete with anyone that season. Even Leigh's Sunoco, despite another subpar year, had a player or two who could play for anyone.

Rather than giving St. Mary's credit, I supported the notion that they took advantage of an unfair system. Why should they be treated differently? In my eyes, those Catholic boys cheated the system, and I am convinced that they did so all these years later. Is it any wonder why I take great satisfaction whenever the Notre Dame Fighting Irish lose a football game?

Game one was four days away, and Wayne decided to hold a practice beforehand. This time he decided to change the way we took batting practice. Rather than pitch batting practice himself, Wayne asked me to do so. Wayne wanted to simulate game conditions, so he asked me to throw as if I was pitching an actual game. On the one hand, it helped our hitters prepare for St. Mary's, but on the other, pitching the whole practice did not help my arm. That night my elbow and shoulder hurt more than they ever had.

My arm still hurt on the day of the game. Each warmup pitch felt like hot needles sticking into my elbow. I simply did not know how long my arm would last. Wayne won the coin toss (tails again!) and I took the mound at the top of the first. I retired the first two batters and then faced my St. Mary's counterpart. Bunky Roberts was one of the best pitchers in the league. After getting ahead in the count, I tried to throw a fastball past him. I threw the ball so hard that my cap fell over my eyes. I heard a crack and looked up to see Bunky rolling in the dirt in obvious pain. My pitch had hit him on his ankle. Unable to put weight on his leg, he was replaced by the St. Mary's manager. I then proceeded to strike out the next batter.

In our half of the inning, we jumped out to a 4-0 lead as the backup St. Mary's pitcher had control problems. Once our batters reached base, we ran the bases like we had done all season. Walks and singles quickly turned into extra bases. We were scoring runs without the benefit of many hits.

I held St. Mary's scoreless through four innings due to the outstanding defense of David and Timmy. Both of them gobbled up hard-hit ground balls. The biggest threat came in the top of the fourth when St. Mary's loaded the bases with two outs. A perfectly timed pickoff throw from Andy to David at third base extinguished the threat.

The St. Mary's manager switched pitchers after three innings, and we found additional success with the reliever. Our lead had stretched to 12-0 entering the final inning. The final inning was one of my most challenging of the season. Each pitch made my elbow throb. My velocity had dropped as well. Unable to rely on a strikeout, I needed to rely on my defense to close out the victory.

St. Mary's scored five runs in the inning. Most of the runs were simply the result of hard-hit balls. The inning should have ended on a ground ball to second, but once again, Davey demonstrated why his defensive skills were best described as "hands of stone." A pop-up to Timmy finally ended the inning and the game. Game one went to us by a final score of 12-5.

Following the game, I immediately went home to ice my arm. But even on the following day, the pain persisted. Over the next couple of days, I did not even bother to play fantasy baseball on my parent's steps. Game two was in two days. Before the game, I would approach Wayne and ask if I could play first base instead. I needed additional time for the flare-up in my elbow and shoulder to subside. Instead, Wayne told me that I would be our starting pitcher. He said he liked the idea of knowing that he had "security" to have me available to pitch the next two games, only needing to win one to become city champions.

"Security." Little did I know then, but security would become my life's work. And much like playing baseball provided me with a lifetime of memories.

Chapter 31
What Now?

Losing the financial freedom that Combat Sports would have provided me, I found myself in a tight bind. The Red Cross laboratory job did not provide much income, and I had a baby at home to take care of. While the $ 2,500 investment to start the business did not sound like a lot, it did represent my life savings.

Fortunately, Roger, my Red Cross boss, volunteered me to serve as the building's night security guard. Red Cross had no luck finding a competent guard service, firing them left and right for a variety of reasons. Examples included guards arriving to work intoxicated, snorting cocaine at their desk, and getting caught having sex with a custodian in the men's room.

My security job consisted of answering after-hour phone calls, responding to freezer alarms, and locking the building at a prescribed time. I would finish my lab job at 4 p.m. and grab a bite to eat, and work the Security desk from 5 p.m. to midnight. On weekends, my hours were longer, 6 a.m. to midnight on Saturdays and 8 a.m. to 10 p.m. on Sundays. The hours were a drag, but the Red Cross paid me well.

After about a month of working these hours, I was getting

exhausted. I knew a schedule change was needed when driving home one Sunday night I slammed on my brakes to avoid hitting the giraffe that had run in front of my car. I guess I was imagining things, but after all these years I am still convinced one of our local zoos was missing a very tall animal.

I went to the Red Cross contracting office the next day intending to resign from my security position. Instead, I was offered a different security position with much fewer hours. I performed this job for the next two years until I resigned from the Red Cross to take a job working for Butch on a government repository contract. Before my departure, I informed the contracting office that I would like to manage their security guard service when they opened their new facility, the Jerome Holland Laboratory in Rockville. But to tell you the truth, I made the offer in jest. I never thought they would take my offer seriously.

Imagine my surprise when three months later, the Red Cross asked me to submit my proposal to provide them with security services. I approached the President of my new company, and he was thrilled to have the Red Cross as a business partner.

When our proposal was accepted, we had three weeks to hire a security staff to provide 24/7 coverage for the new laboratory. It was while I was conducting the first interviews that I came to realize that potential security candidates were often a bit "peculiar." One expressed disappointment learning that the position called for unarmed officers. He told me that he always had a fascination with wanting to shoot somebody. Another presented a resume as thick as a phone book. When I asked him why he had been dismissed from his previous security position, he said it was because he held a knife to the throat of his supervisor. He said he was owed overtime pay and would get his money "No matter what it would take."

The Holland Laboratory opened in December of 1985. A two-story building over a football field long, only one or two laboratories were open for immediate use. Construction workers were still working throughout the facility. It would be nearly a year before work was completed. I was working the day shift once when a very tall white man carrying a huge suitcase was walking towards me in the hallway. He was easily 6'8" and had the biggest afro that I had ever seen. Using my keen security mind, I immediately sensed that he was out of place.

I approached the stranger to ask if he needed assistance. He looked around and whispered, "My name is Anwar Sadat, and I need to speak to President Reagan. But don't tell my wife, she thinks I'm dead."

Holy shit! I found myself face-to-face with an absolute loon. He seriously thought he was the Egyptian President who had been assassinated years earlier. At that point, I had no idea what his intentions were. Was he armed? Why did he need to speak to President Reagan? And was his wife cut up into little pieces in the suitcase he was carrying?

Luckily, I was surrounded by several construction workers, none of whom uttered a word. I felt confident they would come to my aid if needed. Well, at least I hoped they would. Realizing that I needed to get this individual out of the building, I walked him to the main entrance and pointed to a bus sign. I instructed him to tell the bus driver that he needed to go to the White House. He shook my hand and thanked me. As he walked toward the bus stop, I secured the door and never saw him again.

The Holland Laboratory was also the site of another great practical joke. One I thought even rivaled the pig blood football prank. My brother-in-law Bill was one of my part-time officers. I had stopped by the facility to pick him up for a birthday party. His twin four-year-old boys were celebrating a combined birthday party with my son Travis, who was born just a week after them. Bill had rented a gorilla costume to scare the kids at the party.

When I arrived at the facility, I instructed Bill to head down the hallway where the animal facility was located. This facility typically contained rats, mice, and rabbits. I told Bill to put on the gorilla costume and to jump out into the hallway when he heard me cough.

I returned to the security office to await the arrival of Joe, the officer who would be taking over Bill's shift in a few minutes. Joe was an excellent officer who, despite being 87 years old, did not look a day over 75.

Joe was surprised to see me, and I told him I was there to warn him that the National Institutes of Health had mistakenly delivered a gorilla to the Holland Laboratory. The gorilla would remain there until picked up and delivered to his proper location on Monday. I told Joe that I would show him which room the gorilla was located in and that the lights in the room should remain off. Joe seemed apprehensive, especially when I told him that I thought the gorilla's cage looked a bit flimsy.

When we got to around 30 yards from the animal facility, I coughed, and Bill jumped out into the hallway. When looking at the costume up close, you could easily tell it was fake, but from 30 yards away, it looked damn real!

The second Bill jumped out into the hallway, Joe turned and ran in the opposite direction. For a 87-year-old man, he might have broken the world record for the 100-yard dash. He raced out of the building and locked himself inside his truck.

I don't think I had ever laughed so hard in my life. Joe's heart was still pumping fast when he finally realized there was no gorilla. But our prank did raise one serious question. What would we have done had Joe dropped dead of a heart attack? Well, the answer was quite simple. The poor man simply collapsed during the course of his security rounds. What else could we have said?

I was hired as the Protective Services Manager for the National Cancer Institute in 2003. Located at Fort Detrick in Frederick, Maryland, this position proved quite challenging. It was a position I would hold for the next 17 years.

Upon my hire, I immediately walked into a real mess. The security department was in shambles. The former manager had a "closed-door policy," one that he had followed for several years. It was a policy of closing his office door and letting the inmates run the asylum.

My department was understaffed. The number of security shifts was too numerous to count. Some officers only worked 1-2 days a week, while others earned ungodly amounts of overtime pay. I immediately restructured the number of shifts to just five. Three shifts would constitute my full-time guys and two weekend shifts would consist of my part-time officers.

Some of my changes were met with resistance. Some officers complained about losing overtime pay. Others hated the idea of working five days a week. It took some time, but eventually the department came around. Later, two new offsite locations opened, which required 24/7 security coverage. This significantly increased the number of employees in my department. It took some time to get all three locations running smoothly, but I was damn proud of our accomplishments. That said, I still faced challenges. Just like at the Holland Laboratory, I experienced strange individuals. One officer was convinced that I had dressed as a woman to spy on his shift. Another officer expressed concerns that Black Op helicopters were following him home at night. Finally, there was a job interview with a prospective candidate who had previously been employed as an armed officer at a shopping mall. "Troublemakers could leave the mall peacefully or in a body bag. It didn't matter to me which they chose." Needless to say, he was not hired.

It was during the COVID pandemic that I felt my time in security was coming to a close. Several laboratory employees became infected, and consequently, administrative workers began to work from home. My officers were considered essential employees and had to come to work. Many officers resented the fact that when someone tested positive in a laboratory, it was Security officers who had to post "Do Not Enter" signs on doors because most of the Safety employees were "working" from home as well.

Promotions were seemingly granted to employees who kissed ass rather than those who truly deserved them. I refused to play that game. One sycophant was a former officer of mine. He took the meaning of stupidity to an all-new level. Another toady had been let go from another department. Her former supervisor laughed when he heard that she had been rehired. When talk of department reorganization began, I knew my days were numbered. My position was eventually eliminated, and I used my first few months of retirement to recover from total knee replacement. My security career was over.

Chapter 32
Repository Stories

During my 12 years managing the Red Cross security contract, I was also employed as a Facility Manager on a National Institutes of Health National Cancer Institute contract. Our repository provided chemopreventive agents used in cancer prevention research. Our facilty was located in the basement of the building that housed Butch's repository. We were the second government contract awarded to our company. Other contracts would follow in the future, which enabled our company to continue to grow.

Ted was the Principal Investigator of our repository until he moved on to become the company's Director of Quality Assurance a few years later. During the time we worked together, more family members and former Flow Lab employees would also work with us. My sister Barb was our administrative assistant. Bobby Hughes, Dave Vanscoy, and Barb's husband, Bill Dillon came from Flow. Bobby would serve as Ted's assistant, Bill would be a technician, and Dave would later follow Ted to the Quality Assurance Department.

The repository that Butch managed was much more busy than ours. While his contract could generate 200 or more orders a day, our contract only generated a couple. As a result, we often found ourselves with a lot of spare time on our hands.

The 1980s was the heyday of professional wrestling. Hulk Hogan and Andre the Giant ruled the ring. Several of us were wrestling fans and sometimes used our downtime to perfect our wrestling moves. There was a chair right next to the main door of our repository. Individuals returning from lunch often found themselves being jumped on by someone standing on the chair. This juvenile behavior would bother Bobby the most. Once he returned from lunch just as Dave had jumped on my back. Dave pushed me against our office wall, and my ass went right through the drywall. Bobby's face turned beet red. He turned around, got in his car, and drove away. He did not return for hours. Bobby's reaction only made us laugh more.

Barb always had a fear of snakes. One day, while taking a walk at lunch, Ted, Dave, and I captured a large black snake sunning itself on the path. We took the snake back to the repository and put it in Barb's desk. When she returned from lunch, Ted asked her for a paper clip. Just as she opened her desk drawer, the snake sprung out. Barb screamed and ran out of the office. I had never seen her run so fast!

We would play practical jokes on just about anyone. However, since Barb often brought food to feed us, we generally left her alone. Her favorite restaurant was a Chinese place serving delicious dishes in generous portions. Barb would usually bring in leftovers every week. However, after reading one day that the

Health Department had closed the restaurant for having dog carcasses in its walk-in refrigerator, we all began to wonder what Barb had really been feeding us.

Our favorite pastime at the repository was "gentlemen's lunches." That typically meant sneaking out for extra long lunches or going to the local movie theatre to catch a matinee show. Our favorite restaurant was Chesapeake Bay Seafood House. We would go there on a weekly basis to enjoy their all-you-can-eat soup and salad. For $4.99, we would gorge ourselves with a salad and a couple of bowls of soup. Except for Dave. He would eat three helpings of salad and ask if he had time for a fourth. Mind you, the salads were huge! They were served in trough-sized portions. How anyone could eat more than one still amazes me to this day.

All new employees were invited to join the "repository club." To become a member, the new employee had to leap over a packing table. The table was eight feet long, and three feet wide. Most individuals wanting to join the club had to get a running start to clear the three-foot-tall table. One day, our new Assistant Principal Investigator expressed his desire to become a member. Unfortunately, his heels hit the edge of the table, and he face-planted onto the concrete floor. We were convinced that he had killed himself. Luckily, he was not injured, but we made him wait another week before attempting to join our club again.

One of the craziest games we played was seeing who could

avoid heat stroke. Played during the hot summer months, contestants agreed to keep their car windows rolled up, and their air conditioning turned off when departing for the day. The object of the game was to see how far you could drive before succumbing to the heat. It's a wonder we didn't kill ourselves or other innocent people in the process. Boy, were we dumb.

Chapter 33
Championship Series
Game 2

Game two was set for a night game at Dogwood Park. As I began to warm up before the game, we all noticed a change in how our game would be officiated. For the first time all season, two umpires would be present. One would serve as the home plate umpire, while the other would serve as a base umpire. We had never seen either one and were not bothered having a second umpire assigned to our game until they began addressing each St. Mary's player by first name. What in the hell was up with that?

As the coaches met at home plate to swap respective lineup cards, Wayne jokingly asked if either umpire was related to any of the St. Mary's players. Neither took too kindly to his question. As the game progressed, Wayne's question did not seem that far-fetched.

I had an uneasy feeling about the game. The pain in my elbow and shoulder persisted, and I struggled during my pregame warmups. In addition, Bunky had recovered from his ankle injury and was warming up next to the St. Mary's dugout. I suspected the game would be low-scoring. It was during my first inning of pitching that I knew we were in trouble.

To put it kindly, the home plate umpire squeezed the shit out of me. Pitches that Andy and I were certain were catching the corners were called balls. Pitches where Andy did not even have to move his mitt were also called balls. Unless the pitch was right down the middle of the plate, the St. Mary's batters would not swing.

After walking two batters on questionable calls and surrendering a double down the left-field line, we quickly fell behind 2-0. Fortunately, I was able to escape the inning after David snared a line drive with two runners on base. I knew we were in for a long night.

From the second inning on, I simply aimed for the middle of the plate and threw as hard as I could. I was not going to leave a doubt in anyone's mind whether my pitch was a ball or strike. I forced the umpire to call strikes, but in doing so, my elbow screamed for mercy. Not a single St. Mary's player reached base after the first inning.

Unfortunately, Bunky kept our bats quiet as well. We scored our lone run in the bottom of the fourth inning on a sacrifice fly by Andy. The final score was 2-1. The series would go to a third and deciding game. I had two days to get my arm feeling right.

Chapter 34
McBoob

Following my high school graduation, the thought of attending college full-time was simply not appealing to me. Therefore, I accepted a position at Flow Labs working for Cathy while attending junior college at night. I had an absolute blast for the next five years.

We worked in a large repository consisting of over 100 freezers and refrigerators. Several employees helped manage three different National Cancer Institute contracts. These freezers and refrigerators stored biological material used for cancer research. Orders were picked up and shipped daily.

Tony Montiel managed one of the contracts. He was a Cuban refugee who escaped Cuba when Fidel Castro came to power. Tony later participated in the ill-fated Bay of Pigs invasion where he was taken prisoner after promised air support from President Kennedy never materialized. As a result, he absolutely despised JFK!

Tony was a fantastic chess player and would play other players through the mail (this was long before the internet). He would sit at his desk and play several games at once. We would wait until he was lost in concentration before one of us would announce our love of Kennedy. Watching his body begin to twitch and his face turn beet red was always a source of great laughter.

Larry McBrien headed our second cancer contract. Larry was 5'6" and weighed well over 300 lbs. The word that best described his physical appearance was "round." Larry was his own worst enemy. He was constantly doing or saying things that made others think he was a complete moron. Cathy started writing "Larry's Song" as a tribute to him, a written record of every time he said or did something stupid.

On my first day on the job, Larry drove me to the NIH campus to show me where we picked up and delivered orders. While driving to the campus, a Stevie Wonder song blared on the radio. At that moment, Larry turned to me and said, "You know, you could never tell he was blind by the way he sings." I had just heard something to add to the book, and over the next several years, I contributed many more passages to Larry's Song.

By the time I left Flow to take the laboratory position with the Red Cross, Larry's Song had become pretty thick. Hundreds of things that Larry said or did were now recorded for history. I often thought of publishing a book someday. Visions of a Pulitzer Prize and subsequent movie rights flashed in my mind. I kept those notes in my possession for years, occasionally reading some of its passages whenever I needed a laugh. Tragically, the notebook was lost during one of my many moves over the years, its contents were lost forever. It exists now only in my memory. For your reading pleasure, here are some of those memories:

- Larry once called his Project Officer to complain about an order. "Hello Mary, Susan really screwed up this order. She is so damn stupid. Oh, hello, Susan, I thought you were Mary."

- One day, Larry entered the office, sat at his desk, and sighed repeatedly. Finally, one of us took the bait and asked him what was wrong. Larry replied, "My sister is pregnant, and she wouldn't be if she had only used her diagram."

- One summer, many Flow employees decided to go white water rafting on the Cheat River in West Virginia. Some of the employees were concerned that the water level would be so low that there would be no rapids. Jimmy Reynolds, Supervisor of the Glassware Department said, "Don't worry about that. We'll simply throw Larry into the river first. He's so damn big that he'll make the water rise."

- The following year, we returned to the Cheat River, only this time, we went in early April. The water was so cold that the rafting company required you to wear wetsuits. Six of us helped to squeeze Larry into his 8XL suit, my hands disappearing to my wrists in his fat. Afterward, Jimmy had Larry hold a sign that read "Goodyear." Jimmy said, "Larry, with this sort of advertising, we're going to make millions!"

- Each year, the Vice President of Contracts would take us all out to lunch at Chesapeake Bay Seafood House. When the waitress asked Larry for his order, he replied, "I'll take two of all-you-can-eat fried shrimp." When informed that it was an all-you-can-eat buffet, Larry replied, "That's okay; I can eat more with the second plate." When asked for his cocktail order, Larry loudly asked for a "shrimp cocktail."

- Larry treated his parents and sister to an all-expense paid trip to Hawaii one year. When Larry told his Mom that he was considering going too she replied, "No, Larry, you cannot afford it."

- Larry was on the phone trying to speak to one of his customers. "Can I please speak with Dr. Hirshalt..Dr. Hirshalt..Is Dr. Horseshit there?"

- Larry is on the phone again with his Contract Office. "How do you spell that? That's G, as in dog."

- Larry said he preferred to eat brown eggs because they were natural. They hadn't been painted white yet.

- Larry was complaining that he had too many magazines. "I need to cut back on my prescriptions."

- Larry was asked why he never washed his pants. "I don't have to. They are pre-washed jeans."

- Larry talking to Cathy about his favorite radio stations. "I really like green grass music."

- Rod talking about Larry. "If Larry were a fish, he would be easy to catch. He could not turn down the bait."

- Larry came to work with a luggage carrier on top of his car. Jimmy Reynolds replied, "I see you brought your lunchbox to work with you."

- April Fools Day was always a day of fun in the repository. One year we gave Larry the phone number of the National Zoo and informed him that Dr. Lyon had left him a message. About an hour later, we told him that Mr. Foxx had tried to reach him as well. Larry never caught on, even when told later that afternoon by a frustrated zoo employee that "Dr. Geraffe is not available right now. Perhaps you would like to speak to Dr. Elephant instead?"

- Just before my leaving Flow in 1983, tragedy struck the Company. Larry had found Larry's Song! He looked through Cathy's desk one evening and found it. We were all devastated. There was not another copy! When word got out that he had discovered the notebook, Jimmy Reynolds replied, "Well, we have to kill him now."

- Larry brought in a $800 bow and arrow that he purchased to hunt moose in Canada. Mind you, he had never hunted before. The bow sat next to his desk for months, gathering dust. One day Butch grabbed the bow and told Cath to run. She ran into the repository, where she hid behind a chest freezer. Just as she lifted her head to look, an arrow breezed past her head. Butch had come within a fraction of an inch of killing our sister. When asked what would he have told Mom, he said, "Absolutely nothing. I would have dumped her body into the liquid nitrogen tank and eliminated all trace of her."

- Fridays could be boring in the repository because weekend deliveries were rare. To pass the time, we would fill out magazine subscriptions to Larry's home address. We would place bets on who could come up with the best name for the subscription, one that Larry would divulge to all of us after receiving the magazine. Larry McBrain, Larry McBomb, Larry McBum, Larry McMoron, Larry McMud, and Larry McMule were just some of the names we submitted. But the name that upset him the most was Larry McBoob. He came into the office a couple of weeks later and slammed his copy of Highlights on his desk, threatening to strangle the person who was responsible. His reaction only made things worse for him. For the next several days, we would intercept his intercompany mail and change his last name on the envelope to McBoob.

Chapter 35
Championship Series
Game 3

We entered the final game of the series with an overall record of 27-3, 23 more wins than our previous season. F.O. Day had never been city champs, and some thought that just making the championship series was accomplishment enough. We did not feel that way. We wanted more.

The pain in my elbow had not dissipated, and every throw during my warmups hurt like hell. When I saw that the same two umpires were back, I knew my room for error was very small. I told Andy to hold his mitt over the center of the plate, we would not bother messing with the corners.

I retired the side in the top of the first, fanning the last two batters. I led off our half of the inning with a hard-line drive out to the second baseman. Timmy followed with a scorching line drive out to the left fielder. David ended the inning with a deep fly ball run down by the St. Mary's center fielder. We had started the game unlucky. Three hard-hit balls with nothing to show for it.

The second inning ended quickly. I struck out all three batters I faced. In turn, Bunky did the same for St Mary's. In the top of the third, I surrendered the first hit of the game, but the runner was erased by a strong throw by Andy when trying to steal second.

We finally broke through in the bottom of the third without the benefit of a hit. Duck led off and was hit by the pitch. While attempting to steal second base, an errant throw by the St. Mary's catcher allowed Duck to reach third base. Bunky nearly escaped the inning after striking out the next two batters. But while I was at bat, a wild pitch allowed Duck to score the game's first run. At the end of three, we led 1-0.

With just six outs to go, I concentrated on throwing strikes. I struck out the first batter to begin the top of the fourth. The next batter hit a slow ground ball to Davey at second base and the ball rolled through his legs for an error. I struck out the next batter before allowing another ground ball to second. Once again, the ball found the outfield. St. Mary's now had the go-ahead run on first base.

I did not know how much more my elbow could take, but I knew a strikeout would end the inning. I was one pitch away after blowing the first two pitches past him. But when his check swing hit landed near the right field line, my effort was for naught. We now trailed 2-1. The next batter hit a pop fly to second. I pushed Davey out of the way to make the catch myself.

We were retired in order in the bottom of the fourth. I held St. Mary's scoreless in the top of the fifth. Our season came down to our final at-bat. I wish some 53 years later, I could write about our magnificent comeback, how Timmy, Andy, or even Davey hit the game-winning home run. But it was not to be. The final score was 2-1. I finished the game with 13 strikeouts and no walks. St. Marys had collected only two hits. But that was enough. Our miraculous season had come to an end.

After shaking hands with the winning team and returning to our dugout, Mrs. Richardson called out from the stands. "It's okay, Davey. You guys would have won if Tommy pitched better." Dad had to drag Mom to the car. Until the day she died, she always regretted failing to strangle Mrs. Richardson when she had the chance to do so. Wayne congratulated us after the game. He told us how proud he was to be our coach. To the best of my knowledge, he never coached again. The only satisfaction we got was hearing St. Mary's players complain when they learned we were going to Shakey's Pizza to celebrate our season, and they weren't. No one had a bigger smile on their face than Joey.

Chapter 36
A Season Not Over

The final game against St. Mary's was not my last game of the season. Andy and I were chosen to represent Rockville in the Metropolitan Area Baseball Tournament. I reluctantly accepted only after learning that Wayne would be one of our coaches. Like prior All-Star teams, this team consisted primarily of coach's sons, who could hardly play a lick. On the bright side, we were happy that Bobby Puhl would not be on the team.

Wayne only appeared at our first practice and then never again. I later learned that he and his girlfriend decided to go on vacation to Nags Head. I wish he had been present for our second practice.

We had 18 players on our roster, and the head coach decided to have a scrimmage game for our second practice. While my elbow was still bothering me, I quickly learned that I didn't have to be 100% to pitch against these guys. Most of them sucked.

I was the starting pitcher for the scrimmage, and Andy was my catcher. In the second inning the son of the head coach reached third base after a fielding error by our center fielder. He took a big lead off the bag as I delivered my next pitch. Andy then proceeded to throw down to third on a pickoff attempt, but his throw hit the runner on the back of his helmet. The head coach charged out of the dugout and pushed Andy to the ground, screaming at him never to attempt a throw like that again. I was stunned. We had one last practice, and I was not surprised that Andy was a no-show. Our coach had successfully run the best player off our team.

I was the starting pitcher for our first game. I knew we were in trouble when my new catcher asked me not to throw so hard during warmups. I was replaced after throwing two scoreless innings. Our other pitchers did not fare well, as we lost 16-0.

Since it was a double-elimination tournament, I suspected our next game would be our last. I was thankful when the coach told me I would only pitch if needed. I guess after we fell behind 10-0 after the first inning, he did not see the need to use me. Instead, I played most of the game in centerfield, chasing hard-hit balls every inning. The final score was 18-4, my season was finally over.

Perhaps Wayne made the right choice by taking a vacation. I certainly needed one. Miller vacations were by no means exotic but were often quite memorable.

Chapter 37
Vacation Memories

Raising five kids on a Flow Labs salary and a Navy pension did not leave much money for fancy vacations. But Mom and Dad always found ways for family getaways. Whether it was weekend trips to Gettysburg, Pennsylvania, fishing at Great Falls, or visiting out-of-state relatives, these getaways provided a lifetime of memories.

Dad loved to fish. Great Falls and the C&O Canal were just a 30-minute drive from our house so we went there on a frequent basis. Dad would turn on a sprinkler in our backyard in the evening to catch nightcrawlers. Using flashlights, we would catch them as their holes became flooded with water.

I never really enjoyed fishing or became very good at it. I guess that was because of my near death experience at the age of two. Dad had taken us out to Great Falls to fish. As we walked up the towpath to return to our car, no one was paying attention to me. Suddenly, I veered off the towpath and plunged into the canal. Butch recalls seeing my entire body become submerged before Dad told him to jump in and save my dumb ass. Butch said I was only in the water for a few seconds, but I can still recall all these years later, my lungs rapidly filling with water. I'm shocked that I did not require CPR. No wonder I never shared Dad's passion for fishing.

Dad no doubt inherited his love of fishing from his mother. There was never a fish too small to keep in Grandma Miller's eyes. Hell, she would eat a baby bluegill if you let her.

One of my fondest memories is fishing with Grandma at Great Falls. Catfish were the only fish that Dad never kept. Evidently, they were too much of a pain in the ass to clean. So when my brothers or I would catch one, we would show it to Grandma. "That's good eating," she would always say before cussing us out when we would throw the catfish back in the water.

One summer, our family vacationed on Beaver Island in Michigan. I was only four, but the memory of that vacation still haunts me. First, to get on the island, you had to board a ferry. This would be the first time I ever experienced seasickness. I heaved my guts over the railing for the entire 32-mile choppy waters voyage to the island. Ted would later tell me that wasn't as bad as the kid he watched eating black licorice and spinning in circles before the ferry started out. That kid would later vomit all over his white tee shirt. It is probably a good thing that I was later rejected by the U.S. Navy. To this day, I cannot even stand on a dock without feeling queasy.

My other Beaver Island nightmare involved snakes. During the day, I enjoyed playing on the beach. But at night, snakes would come out of Lake Michigan and slither onto the sand. You could not walk on the beach at night without stepping on one. One night, Butch thought he was hilarious after he caught a snake and told me that I could pet it. As my finger approached the snake's head, Butch released his hold on the snake, and it bit me. I can still picture the snake's mouth engulfing my index finger up to the knuckle.

Unfortunately, this would not be my last terrifying experience with a snake. A couple of years later, Dad, Butch, and Ted returned from a fishing trip with a tee shirt wrapped in a knot. "Hey Tommy, we caught some frogs for you." Just as I untied the knot, a four-foot black snake sprang out. I nearly shit myself as Dad and my brothers laughed hysterically.

Some of my fondest memories involved visiting Dad's relatives in western Pennsylvania. His older brother and two younger sisters lived in a small town called Guys Mills. Uncle Paul lived in a dilapidated house that scared the hell out of me. The house was infested with rats and mice. He kept live chickens in his basement. His German Shepherd, Killer, always sat by his side. Killer would growl and bare his teeth whenever someone got near him.

We tried to limit the time we spent at Uncle Paul's house, but on occasion, we would spend the night. For Barb and Cath, rats and mice in the house were the least of their concerns. Far worse, they were forced to sleep with their cousins, all of whom were notorious bedwetters. The smell of urine always filled the bedroom air. Barb is still traumatized from the time when one cousin gorged herself eating green apples and subsequently shit herself in bed.

Some of our Guys Mills cousins were a bit shoddy. One became a home builder who erected several houses throughout Guys Mills. Unfortunately, his craftsmanship and dubious business dealings eventually led him to flee to Montana. His younger brother was thrown in prison after robbing the country store. Since Guys Mills was such a small town, everyone knew each other by first name. That made his decision to rob the place without bothering to wear a mask a bit more strange.

Some of our Guys Mills cousins did get to fool us city folk. Butch recalls walking with them down a country road and coming across a field of cows. He could see that the field was enclosed by an electric wired fence. Our cousins dared Butch to touch it. No self-respecting member of the Dare Devil Club could turn down a dare. Butch touched the wire with a stick, and nothing happened. He was then dared to pee on it. Butch was President of the Dare Devil Club. His position and reputation were at stake. The dare was once again accepted! The subsequent immediate shock of electricity halted his peeing and knocked Butch on his ass. Our cousins thought it was the funniest thing they had ever seen.

Years later, while working at the Holland Laboratory, I was wearing my Pittsburgh Pirates cap when I was approached by a young Red Cross employee. She asked if I was from Pittsburgh. I said no but that my father was from the area. When she asked me what town, I told her Meadville. "Oh yes, I know where Meadville is," she replied. I then asked her if she ever heard of Guys Mills. Imagine my surprise when she said, "Oh my god! I dated a guy from Guys Mills!" I sure hope it wasn't one of my cousins.

Chapter 38
A New Season

The following year, I advanced to play in the Rockville Boys Baseball Midget Division. The only real difference was the pitching rubber was a foot farther from home plate. While this distance did not adversely affect my pitching or velocity, I knew my arm was not the same. Several of our players from the previous year had moved on to different teams or had stopped playing altogether. Timmy chose to play for a County team coached by a Twinbrook school teacher and David had returned to bowling full-time. Thankfully, I still had Andy as my catcher.

Our new coach was Gerald Wright, also a former Marine. Unlike Wayne, he did not have long hair or a beard. He was a construction worker with arms like Hercules. He was one intimidating man. Our assistant coach was Billy Baker, who had once had a tryout with the Pittsburgh Pirates. He would serve as our pitching coach.

A couple of older kids were on the team, and they expected to be our primary pitchers. But during our first practice, I threw the bulk of batting practice, then again during a practice game that the coaches had scheduled with another team. The older players appeared to resent that decision.

Things got even more complicated when I was chosen to be our opening-day starter against Hot Shoppes. As in the previous year, we handled them relatively easily, beating them by the score of 12-2. I finished with nine strikeouts. At our next practice, two of our players quit the team. Both were upset with our coach's decision to name me the starting pitcher. I suspected that meant I would be counted upon to do the bulk of the pitching.

However, Billy proved to be a godsend to me. He knew our team was not very talented and refused to pitch me every game. He planned to use other players to pitch regularly, allowing me to rest my arm as much as possible. I later learned that Billy's baseball career ended after he severed nerves in his pitching arm in a car accident. Despite this injury, I have never seen someone throw a baseball as hard as he could.

For the third consecutive year, I was chosen to represent our team in the annual All-Star game. Our other team representative was our first baseman, Alan, a tall, gangly kid who was just plain awful. I don't think he got a hit all season, and his fielding was atrocious. I recall an instance when I threw over to first in a pick-off attempt. I had the base runner dead to rights, but Alan never moved his glove. My throw struck him in the face, and he collapsed on the ground. Visions of Coach Wayne flashed in my mind. Luckily, Alan only suffered a black eye.

I never understood why Coach Wright chose Alan for the All-

Star team. I suspect it was because Alan had a very attractive mom with whom Coach constantly flirted. Nevertheless, his decision caused a lot of resentment on the team. The one player who deserved to be selected soon quit.

We only won a few games that season, but we had fun. Our lowest point of the season was suffering another loss to Optimist, so we had to carry that monkey on our backs for another season. Not having to pitch every game saved additional wear and tear on my arm. I hoped to pitch a bit more the next season, and I expected our record would improve. Well, I was right about one thing.

Chapter 39
Redemption! Well, Not Quite

Things did not go exactly as planned the following season. Coach Billy had moved to California, and I was the only pitcher on the team who could throw strikes. We dropped our first ten games of the year, often by lopsided scores.

The pain returned to my elbow, and I could no longer throw hard consistently. In some games, I had virtually no pain, while I struggled from the outset in others. Amazingly, our losing streak finally ended against the most unlikely of teams, our archnemesis Optimist. But it was how it ended that caused great controversy on the team.

Coach Wright had no assistant coaches during our second season. When he had to go out of town for a funeral, he needed to find an adult to cover during his absence. That person turned out to be my brother Butch.

Coach Wright asked Butch to coach our team and said that the lineup card had already been made. Butch just had to be there for supervision. Butch agreed but failed to inform Coach Wright about one thing.

Just before we took the field against Optimist a couple of days later, Butch introduced himself to the team and then proceeded to tear up the lineup card. He announced that if he was going to coach, he would make "His own damn lineup." I knew instantly that I was screwed.

I had been scheduled to be the starting pitcher. Instead, Butch penciled me in for left field. Andy, who had never pitched a game in his life would be our new starting pitcher. Butch then proceeded to move players to various positions, some that the player had never played before.

As Andy warmed up, Butch simply told him to throw strikes. Andy was not to worry about using a fancy windup or worry about comments from the Optimist players. Butch's decision proved to be a wise one. Andy used his strong arm to mow down Optimist batters.

We proceeded to play our best game of the year. Late in the game, we held a two-run lead but Optimist had runners on second and third. The next batter hit a line drive single to left that I fielded on one hop. When the Optimist runner on second tried to score, I threw him out at home plate, preserving our one-run lead. Butch then handed me the ball to close out the game. I threw two shutout innings, and we defeated Optimist for the first time in years.

When Coach Wright returned to our next practice, he was not a happy camper. I do not know what bothered him the most, Butch having ripped up his lineup or hearing my teammates telling him that they wanted Butch as their new coach. Either way, few words were spoken between us during that practice.

I was named to the All-Star team for a fourth consecutive season, along with our third baseman Timmy Clifford. Timmy only played one season, but he was a really good player. Our opponents often made fun of his long hair that he wore in a ponytail.

I started the game in center field. In the bottom of the first inning, I led off with a walk. Following my steal of second base, Timmy, drove me home with a hard-hit single to left. The score remained 1-0 until the last inning.

Coach Wright sat with my parents during the game and hoped that our one-run lead would stand. Since we were not having a very good season, Coach Wright hoped that his players would at least be responsible for an All-Star Game victory. Unfortunately, our opponent scored three runs in their last at-bats to secure the victory.

Sadly, Timmy died of a heroin overdose a few years after graduating from high school. He was found in his car outside a Rockville bar with the needle still in his arm. I often wonder how things could have been different had he concentrated on an athletic career instead of turning to drugs.

The highlight of our season was our matchup with St. Mary's. Once again, they were one of the best teams in the league, and we were a bottom dweller. I was our starting pitcher. My arm felt pretty good due to my desire to beat them.

I pitched my best game of the year. The lead seesawed back and forth. While the St. Mary's coach made several pitching changes; I pitched a complete game. We held a two-run lead heading into the final inning. Then, with two outs and two runners on base, I enticed the batter to hit a lazy fly ball to right field, directly to the reliable fielding Duck Gavin. I prematurely leaped for joy, only to watch Duck drop the ball. The batter raced to third. The game was now tied. I composed myself and struck out the next batter to end the inning.

Needing one run to win the game, our shortstop, Butchie Turner, led off in the bottom of the 5th inning. After taking a called third strike, Butchie flung his bat towards our dugout, almost kneecapping me in the process. The umpire immediately ejected him from the game.

We now faced a major dilemma. Having started the game with just nine players, we would not be able to continue the game into extra innings, playing only eight. We needed to score or face losing by forfeit. After Andy and I both struck out, the forfeit became official.

I sat on our bench in total despair. Losing a game in that manner stunned all of us. Losing to St. Mary's again just made it worse. However, the St. Mary's head coach did earn my respect when he sought me out after the game. He shook my hand and said my pitching performance was the best he had seen all year.

I would have one last chance to get my revenge against St. Mary's. But that time would not come until many years later.

Chapter 40
Time to Hang It Up

At season's end, I was unable to sleep many nights because of the constant pain in my arm. I finally asked Mom to take me to Bethesda Naval Hospital, where I was diagnosed with tendinitis in my elbow and a strained rotator cuff. I thought the doctor was joking when he advised me to stop pitching. Forever.

Before the start of the next season and after experiencing pain once again while playing catch with Andy, I made the difficult decision to sit out the season. I hoped a complete year of rest would help my arm. I planned to play Rockville Junior League ball and then try out for my high school team as a sophomore.

Unfortunately, my baseball career ended in the 9th grade. By that time, I had given up pitching altogether. Coach Wright started me in right field, where I would only use my arm when trying to throw out runners trying to go from first to third on singles hit to me. Our team still was not very good, but at least we had fun.

We had an afternoon game at Welsh Park. In the top of the first, a batter hit a sinking line drive to right center. I dived for the ball, landing on my right side, then rolled over, racking myself in the process. I lay on the field, convinced I had broken a rib while thinking at the same time that my balls were in my throat. I was even more upset that I dropped the damn ball!

At the end of the inning, I slowly made my way to our bench, feeling extreme pain when I tried to breathe. I was scheduled to bat leadoff and dropped the bat in agony while taking a practice swing. I told Coach Wright I did not think I could continue playing. He looked at me and said, "We only have nine players, Miller. Do you want us to forfeit?" He told me to step up to the plate and just stand there. I did not have to swing the bat.

To my utter disappointment, the pitcher walked me on four pitches. I slowly jogged to first hoping my balls would descend soon. Upon reaching the bag, I was shocked to see Coach Wright signal me the steal sign. My teammates began laughing on the bench. I had always taken pride in my running ability, and usually led my team in stolen bases. But in this instance, I was thrown out by 20 feet. By this time, Coach Wright was laughing as well. Perhaps this was his way for getting even for Butch tearing up his lineup two years earlier.

We finished the season near the bottom of the league. It would take years for my arm to feel healthy again. When I blew out my knee a few months later, my career was over. I never played baseball again.

Chapter 41
Elvis Has Left The Building

Fans of Elvis Presley will recognize August 16, 1977, as the day he died at the age of 42. This was also the day that I started my first job as a movie usher at White Flint Mall. It proved to be a rewarding experience for me especially since it lessened the blow of being unable to participate on my high school athletic teams.

Unlike many friends, I did not desire to work at a fast food establishment. Perhaps that was because of Ted's extremely short tenure in doing so. Upon arriving on his first day of work at McDonalds, his first assignment was to mop the floor. Just as he started to mop the floor, his 18-year-old supervisor informed him that he was doing it wrong. Before he could explain to Ted what the problem was, Ted dropped the mop and walked out of the restaurant. His McDonalds career lasted five minutes.

Having been a movie buff for as long as I can remember, working as an usher was very enjoyable. White Flint consisted of five screens. During the time I worked there, I was able to watch many movies for free. My friends appreciated the free passes I gave them on a regular basis.

My first day on the job was one to remember. Star Wars was the most popular movie at the time. Huge lines would form before the theater even opened, and shows sold out on a daily basis. Upon my arrival for my first day, I was paired with another usher who would serve as my trainer. Within minutes, we were facing an angry mob.

White Flint movie projectionists were expected to rewind their movies after each night's performances, but as I was to find out, one of the projectionists had failed to do so. He waited to begin the rewind process until his arrival to work that day. Rather than remaining in his booth, he entered another booth to play poker with a fellow projectionist. When he returned to his booth 20 minutes later, he opened the door to see hundreds of feet of film pile onto the lobby floor. During the rewind process, the film split in the middle, and he was not in the booth to catch it. The film was destroyed, and that day's showing of Star Wars had to be canceled.

Our Manager instructed my trainer and me to go outside of the theatre and "quietly" inform patrons that Star Wars could not be shown that day. We were to offer free passes to those who had been waiting to see it. Our attempt to keep the cancellation notice quiet failed miserably. The first person we talked to immediately began shouting obscenities at us.

Within seconds, chaos erupted. We were pushed against the

wall as irate individuals threatened us with bodily harm. My life flashed before my eyes as I was convinced that I was about to die accepting a job that only paid $2.30 an hour. Thankfully, our lives were saved when White Flint Mall security officers pulled us away from the hostile crowd.

The mid-70s was when Farrah Fawcett-Majors became America's favorite sex symbol. White Flint Movies celebrated her status by running a double-feature midnight show highlighted by her first "nudie" role. Majors played a small role in the 1970 film Myra Breckinridge, which was considered very risque upon its release. Nowadays, I suspect the same film would be rated PG-13.

Every pervert in the Washington Metropolitan area seemed to show up for the midnight show. And I was the lucky one chosen to be the closing usher that evening. Individuals who purchased tickets for the show arrived carrying beer and liquor bottles. Many were already extremely intoxicated. Over 30 cases of beer were confiscated at the door! It would prove to be a long night.

Individuals expecting to see a nude Farrah were in for a rude awakening. If one blinked, they were liable to miss her during the one nude scene she had in the movie. Once many patrons realized that the movie was not X-rated, they streamed into the lobby demanding their money back. I became the focus of their ire after my Manager failed to leave her office to face them.

One customer, in particular, caught my eye. He was a huge man, easily 6'6" and weighing close to 300 lbs. Before the start of the movies, he flung open the theater door just as another man carrying several buckets of popcorn was about to enter. Popcorn flew everywhere as he knocked the buckets to the ground. Instead of apologizing, he simply chuckled and walked by. I had a feeling that I had not seen the last of him.

The movies ended around 4 a.m. Most of the people had long left the theatre. I was standing at the top of the ramp as the few remaining patrons departed, one being the same large man I just described. As he walked out the exit door, he looked at me and said, "Those movies were so damn bad that I ripped my chair from the floor."

After the theatre had emptied, I went to investigate his claim. And sure enough, his seat was laying in the middle of the aisle. He had ripped it out of the concrete with his bare hands. All I could think was that was a helluva lot better than him doing the same thing to me!

Remember when I wrote that my first day working at the theater was the same day that Elvis died? Well, three months later, the General Manager of White Flint decided to hire an Elvis impersonator to perform a live midnight concert. Set to appear on a Friday and Saturday night, the shows sold out within minutes.

Luckily, I was not the closing usher for this fiasco. While not an Elvis fan myself, I stuck around to watch the show. At $25 a ticket, a nice chunk of change in 1977, the audience was expecting a professional performance. That would certainly not be the case.

The show was supposed to start at midnight, but the band began to play at 12:30 a.m. Elvis was not yet present. After playing one song, the audience politely clapped, but their patience began to wear thin when the band repeated the same tune.

I guess I was responsible for instigating the crowd when I cried, "We want Elvis!" Within seconds, many patrons began shouting the same thing. Finally, 45 minutes late, Elvis suddenly appeared. He ran down the aisle wearing a silver jumpsuit. He was about 5'2" and tipped the scales at well over 200 lbs.

His first song was Hound Dog, and the crowd was stunned. Though a few people clapped, many walked up the aisle to ask for their money back. This guy could not sing a lick.

Both my Manager and General Manager hid inside a projectionist booth. The money had long been deposited, and refunds were not being issued. Luckily, I had removed my uniform and was not recognized as a theatre employee. The closing usher was left to fend for himself as he was surrounded by the angry mob. Better him than me! All these years later, I can still vividly recall the husband, wife, and their two teenage children sitting in the lobby dejectedly as the father cried out, "He doesn't look or sound like Elvis," as tears streamed down his face.

The most amazing thing to me was the nerve of the impersonator having the guts to return for his Saturday performance. Many of the Friday night patrons had purchased tickets for the second show. While many simply did not come, those that did came for the express purpose of hassling the hell out of the impersonator. He could hardly be heard as the audience made fun of his appearance and lack of talent. I often wonder if his career as an Elvis impersonator ended that night. For his sake, I sure hope it did.

I worked at the theatre for over a year and left to accept the position at Flow. Before my departure, I helped one of my theatre buddies pull off a funny prank before he left for college.

I was the closing usher one night. My friend and another theatre employee left after the final movies started. But instead of going home, they reentered White Flint Mall at the Security entrance by the movie's emergency exit doors. I let them in, and they waited inside the theatre as the last film ended.

I walked out of the theatre with my Manager. We both got into our cars and left the parking lot. Unbeknownst to her, I drove back to the mall and entered through the same Security entrance. I knocked on the theatre door, and my two buddies let me in.

We removed a ladder from the custodial closet and proceeded to unscrew every lightbulb in the theatre lobby. Not wanting to be malicious, we did not steal the lightbulbs. Instead, we made sure that each bulb was hanging by a thread.

I was scheduled to work when the theatre opened the following day. When my Manager turned on the lights, the lobby remained dark. After checking the electrical panel, she notified the mall electrician. He lived over an hour away, and it was supposed to be his day off.

While waiting for the electrician to arrive, she instructed a new usher to get the ladder and replace the bulbs with new ones. She thought that 50 bulbs had all blown at once.

The usher replaced 15-20 bulbs before finally realizing that none of them were screwed in properly. What a dummy! When he notified the Manager, she realized she had been pranked. She turned to me and said, "I know exactly who did this!" She said the name of another usher who was not well-liked. "I bet you're right!" I replied. The mall electrician was not happy upon his arrival.

Chapter 42
Does My Record Still Stand?

By the time I entered high school, I was the last Miller sibling living at home. Barb and Cath had married, and both Butch and Ted had long moved out, both working full-time at Flow Labs with Dad. Mom was basically worn out raising my siblings, so she allowed me to do whatever I wanted.

I always got good grades, so my folks were happy as long as I continued to do so. Mom knew that I missed playing baseball. The pain in my elbow and shoulder would take years to subside, and the recovery from my knee surgery was a long process. So whenever I asked to skip school to work on class papers from home or to work extra hours at the theatre, she rarely objected.

Despite being a hero to the pot community at my high school, I never did drugs. And unlike Dad, I never smoked either. I admit I did my share of underage drinking, but I blame Mom for that. After all, she was the same woman who once chased after the beer wagon at the conclusion of a Flow Labs company picnic. As long as I did not drink and drive, she didn't care if I had a beer or two. The 70s was also a different era. Most of my friends were heavy beer drinkers. Fortunately for them, heavy crackdowns on drunk drivers did not occur until a few years later. Beer drinking or not, that's not to say I didn't get into trouble from time to time. In fact, I think I may still hold the distinction of being the only person ever kicked out of a miniature golf course and a bowling alley on the same weekend.

When I worked at the White Flint movie theatres, I spent most of my spare time with coworkers. A nearby Putt Putt miniature golf course was a popular get-together attraction. Every Friday night, you could play from midnight to 6 a.m. for just $5. Hundreds of people would attend this event, with more than a few being intoxicated upon their arrival.

One night several of us from the theatre arrived to play. After playing a couple of rounds, we began to place bets. Each of us bet a dollar to see who would have the lowest score at each hole. If no one won, the bet would carry over and increase at the next hole. The minimum wage was only $2.30 an hour at that time. So as the pot increased, so did our competitive juices.

When the pot reached $30, it represented a nice chunk of change because that's what most of us made in a week's work. After my buddies missed their putts on one particular hole, I only had to sink a three-foot putt to collect the money. But to my bitter disappointment, the ball rimmed out of the hole, and our competition continued. Out of frustration, I slammed my putter against the railing of the hole we had just completed. I honestly thought the railing was made of wood. So imagine my surprise when the metal railing rang out with a rather loud "TWANG!!!!"

Within seconds my friends and I were confronted by the Putt Putt manager, who instructed us to vacate the course. Evidently, we had been having too much fun and the loud noise that I had just created finally wore out his patience. I can't remember if any of us had been drinking. But I won't ever forget losing out on the money because I couldn't make a damn three-foot putt!

Several years later, I would actually play a round of real golf. Many of my softball buddies had been golfers for years. I would constantly tease them for playing an "old man's game." I guess they finally got tired of my mouth and scheduled a date for me to join them.

I had previously been to driving ranges and was well aware of how difficult golf was. Knowing that I was about to embarrass myself, I insisted that we reserve the earliest tee-off time possible. I figured the fewer golfers on the course to see me, the better.

When we arrived for our 5:25 a.m. tee-off, one of my friends handed me a bag of old golf balls. "Here, you can lose these," he said.

His words proved prophetic. Simply put, I was plain awful. My drives never found the green. Balls were lost in the woods or veered way off course. I was so bad that I stopped bothering to keep score.

As we reached the tenth green, I was discouraged to see that we had returned to the clubhouse. Older golfers were drinking their morning coffee as I prepared to tee off. I suddenly felt pressure when I heard one of them say, "Look! It's a lefty!" As I turned around, I saw I had an audience of 25-30 golfers surrounding me. For the only time all day, I hit a nice drive. The ball traveled high and straight for about 125 yards, disappearing over the hill. Several golfers clapped their approval. None of them saw my next shot I shanked into a pond.

The 16th hole was a par three. My second shot landed in weeds three feet tall, about 30 yards from the hole. I told my buddies, "Take out the flag. This one is going in." I took out my putter and smacked the ball. It went straight up, bounced two times, and dropped into the cup. I shot par for the hole and quit for the day. I refused to play the last two holes. I never played golf again.

The night following the Putt-Putt incident, we tested our skills at bowling, and it proved to be a night to remember. I suck at bowling. No matter how hard I rolled a ball or where I aimed the ball, I rarely rolled a strike. In fact, on most occasions, I would leave only a pin or two standing. And no matter how hard I tried, I rarely completed the spare.

On this particular night, I constantly had spare opportunities. My ball would seemingly hit the pocket in the perfect location, only to leave a pin standing. Finally, I told my friends, "If I leave a pin standing this time, I'm going to run down the lane and kick the damn thing down!"

Sure enough, my subsequent roll succeeded in knocking down just nine pins. In a rage, I stepped over the line to make my way down the lane and was immediately grabbed by two bowling alley Nazis.

I was taken to the manager's office where, for the next 45 minutes, I was threatened to be handed over to the police. The manager lectured me about the oil used in each bowling lane and how disturbing this oil affected how the bowling balls traveled toward the pins. Who knew?

Needless to say, the bowling alley manager took his job seriously. His knowledge of oil, lanes, bowling balls and pins was quite impressive. After a while, I began to wonder if he was David's Dad. Maybe he was the reason why David stopped playing baseball to concentrate on his bowling career instead.

Finally, after hearing everything there was to know about the great sport of bowling, the manager decided not to call the police. However, since I had "severely damaged" the integrity of the bowling lane, I was asked to leave the alley and barred from returning for one month.

I never bowled again.

Chapter 43
Softball Days

Following my knee surgery after my sophomore year, I was not able to run until March of my junior year. I struggled to regain my range of motion in my knee, and it never increased beyond 110 degrees. Knowing that I could never pass a sports physical to play high school baseball, I instead chose to play with Butch in the Rockville Men's Softball League

League rules stipulated that you first had to be a high school graduate to be eligible to play. Instead, I and a couple high school buddies snuck onto the team while still juniors. No one seemed to care because our team was pretty bad, but starting the following year and continuing for 19 more years, our teams usually contended for division titles.

I began to manage our team in 1978. Managing consisted of two things: determining the batting order, and making sure players knew when it was their turn to provide post-game refreshments. Over the years, we would gain a reputation as a team that enjoyed a few cold beers after each game. Okay, more than a few. On occasion, I may have had to manage some players who had a few before the game even started.

One of our biggest rivals was a team consisting of Montgomery

County police officers. For a profession that is supposed to treat individuals professionally and with respect, these guys were some of the most arrogant people I have ever met. Tempers usually flared whenever we played them.

The first time we played them, they entered the game undefeated. They typically beat teams with ease, so they were surprised when we took and maintained an early lead. Entering the last inning, we held a one-run lead.

The police team had the tying run on first. I was playing shortstop. The next batter hit a ground ball to me. A force out at second would end the game. But to my chagrin, I booted the ball, which placed the winning run on first with their best batter stepping to the plate. When he launched a long drive to left, thoughts of being the goat of the game raced through my head. But to my complete joy, our left fielder made an incredible catch to end the game.

Rather than congratulate us at the end of the game, many of the police players refused to shake our hands. Those that did called us lucky and wished us Merry Christmas instead.

The following year, we faced the police team again. It was clear from the outset that they were looking for revenge. We kept the game close and took the lead when I scored from third on a short flyball to center. The throw home was almost perfect, but my hand touched the plate before the catcher tagged me. That call resulted in the centerfielder practically losing his mind, believing I was out.

The same centerfielder tried to stretch out a single hit to left field in the following inning. Playing shortstop once again, I took the throw from my outfielder and applied a sweep tag on the runner. Unfortunately, my tag missed him by a good two feet as I presented the ball to the home plate umpire. Had the umpire bothered to move from the plate, he would have seen that I had missed the tag. Instead, not having the proper angle to see the tag, the umpire called the runner out. The runner went berserk, screaming at the umpire that I had failed to tag him. I guess I didn't help matters when I told him that I had. Memories of tormenting Bobby Puhl came to mind when the umpire finally ejected him. Only this time, this player probably had a gun in his car. I should have kept my mouth shut.

One of my fondest softball memories did not even include a game. Butch had a large safe in his repository that was used for the storage of controlled drugs. When that contract ended, the safe was made available to anyone who wanted to purchase it.

For the bargain price of $50, Dad purchased the safe to store some of his stamp collection. Standing about six feet tall and two feet wide, the damn thing weighed several hundred pounds.

Dad enlisted the help of the softball team to move the safe into his house. But he wasn't content to just get it into the house. He wanted the safe to be placed in the basement. It had taken our entire team to lug the safe into the house. Getting it down the basement was another problem altogether.

Leather straps were placed around the safe. Several 2'x4' boards were placed over the basement steps. While eight members of the team held the straps, two of us went in front of the safe to help to glide it down the boards.

Just as the safe started its path down the steps, my teammate Rick said, "If those straps snap, we're dead." Personally, I did not consider that a problem. I was convinced the stairs would collapse first. But I did wonder how we got chosen to be the ones in front of the safe.

Luckily, the safe reached its final resting place. It remained in the basement for years. When Cathy sold the house years after my parents' deaths, the safe conveyed.

My favorite memories of playing softball remain being Butch's teammate all those years. I had grown up watching him play on the Flow Labs teams and having him as my teammate for over 20 years provided me with a lifetime of pleasant memories. Except for the time I wanted to kill him.

After experiencing a dreadful first year playing together, our 1978 team was the start of several successful seasons. After we had won our end-of-the-season tournament, the league director invited our team to participate in a one-pitch tournament consisting of the very best teams in Rockville.

A one-pitch game is exactly how it is described. A pitcher threw a single pitch to each batter he faced. If the batter swung and missed or if he did not take a swing and the pitch was called a strike, he was out. If the pitch was called a ball, the batter took first base. Foul balls were also outs. As a result, games sped quickly and typically ended in around 30 minutes. Successful teams were those who had pitchers who could throw consistent strikes.

Butch was our pitcher, and he was convinced that he would do well. We accepted the invitation from the league director. It was a double-elimination tournament, and our first game was played on a Saturday morning.

True to his word, Butch pitched great. With big brother consistently throwing strikes, we easily won our first game. Following a 30-minute break, we won our second game as well. When we reported our victories to the league director, a look of amazement appeared on his face. It was only then that he confessed that he invited us to play simply to fill out the tournament bracket. He was convinced that the other teams in the tournament were better than us.

We played two more games at noon and 1:00 p.m. and were victorious in both. Once again the league director seemed shocked by our success.

Our fifth game of the day was scheduled for late afternoon. We had over three hours to rest. Instead, Butch and another teammate decided to go to the Crab Shack for lunch and a beer. Upon their return, it quickly became apparent that Butch had imbibed a few beers too many.

Our game turned ugly quickly. No doubt seeing two catchers instead of one, Butch could not throw a strike if his life depended upon it. Walk after walk led to numerous runs scored against us. I was playing shortstop, and I seethed as the onslaught continued. I had finally seen enough when after fielding a ball hit to him, Butch threw the ball 20 feet over the head of our first baseman with the ball landing in a creek. As team manager, I had no option but to bench my big brother.

Following our loss, we returned the next day to complete the tournament. By that time Butch had regained his sobriety, and we did well. We advanced to the semi-finals before losing by a single run.

Over the years, Butch would claim that he must have eaten a bad crab and that he was suffering from food poisoning. But I know better. My childhood sports idol had screwed us. And I have never let him forget that.

Our most intense game occurred late in my softball career. By that time, we were easily the oldest team in the league. Most of my teammates had played together for 15+ years. It was the final game of the regular season, and we had already clinched first place. The last game was meaningless.

Our opponent was the second-place team whom we had already defeated handily earlier in the season. Most of their players were in their mid-20s or younger. I suspect they were a bit taken back by our success.

The game was scheduled to begin at 7:00 p.m. That meant most of our players had 2-3 hours to kill after they had left work. That also meant most of them had a few drinks before game time.

Before the game began, we decided to change positions. For the first time since my little league days I pitched. Butch played left field for the first time in several years. Other teammates played positions they had never played before.

The first inning proved a bit ugly for us. I surrendered ten runs before the inning ended. A bases loaded fly ball to Butch should have ended the inning, but the ball landed 20 feet behind him. He later admitted to seeing three balls instead of one. Roger, our regular starting pitcher, tried to field a hard ground ball by first crossing his legs to protect his genitalia. Needless to say, pregame refreshments had taken its toll.

As their lead stretched to 15 runs, tempers began to flare. Our opponent was upset that we were not taking the game seriously. To make matters worse, we began to try the patience of the umpire. On several occasions he had to warn our catcher to get rid of the lit cigar in his mouth.

Things turned worse after Butch slid into second base to breakup a double play. The shortstop who had taken the throw shoved Butch. Luckily we got Butch off the field before punches were thrown. As Butch walked off the field he had a few choice words to the shortstop. By this time, I had sobered up and told Butch to shut up. The umpire then warned both teams that any further incident would result in a forfeit.

As we took the field to start the next inning, we were down a player. Evidently Butch was upset that his kid brother had yelled at him and decided to walk home. On his journey home he walked into the house of one of our former teammates, Kenny, who was home recovering from knee surgery. Kenny now played for the team that we played that night. Butch told him that his team was a bunch of assholes and then helped himself to a few beers from his fridge. Kenny would later say that he thought Butch would never leave.

Chapter 44
Redemption

I would go on to coach both of my kids in sports. My son, Travis, played basketball and baseball. My daughter, Taylor, played softball in high school. I have fond memories of coaching them, in addition to occasional nightmares.

Taylor's best sport was track and field. She was an accomplished long-distance runner and competed in the City of Rockville's Youth Track Program. Unfortunately, her high school did not have a track and field team. When she asked if she could try out for the softball team, I was curious as to how well she would do.

I thought Taylor would be out of her element since she had never played softball before. I was dead wrong about that. Taylor quickly became one of the best players on the team. And for two years, I was the team's scorekeeper and assistant coach.

Very few of the girls on the team even wanted to play. Many joined the team because they liked the idea of early class dismissal for away games. Those who wanted to play simply lacked talent. Some refused to field groundballs for fear of breaking their nails. I often drove the team bus for away games.

The conversations I overheard from those teenage girls still make the hair on the back of my neck rise. Sometimes, I wonder in amazement how I did not drive off the road in utter shock.

The head coach of the team was a very nice lady. Unfortunately, she wasn't much of a coach. She insisted on playing only her upperclassmen and rarely played her younger players. This might have made sense if her upperclassmen were any good. But that clearly wasn't the case.

Our starting shortstop was a senior who batted third, and I don't think she got a hit the entire season. Worse yet, she proved to be a sieve in the field. On the rare occasions she actually fielded a ball, her throws to first base were rarely on target. Our starting pitcher had some talent but was more interested in adding to her career strikeouts total than actually trying to win games.

Saint James was the one team in the league that we could beat. While our pitcher could actually throw strikes; their pitchers simply could not. All our batters had to do was stand at the plate and await the inevitable base on balls.

We played Saint James late in the year, and our head coach was excited at the prospect of finally winning a game. We jumped to a huge lead as the Saint James pitcher walked batter after batter. Our head coach encouraged our players not to swing the bat as our lead grew to an incredible 25 runs. I had seen enough. I instructed our batters to swing at any close pitch. With the slaughter rule not coming into play until the 3rd inning; we would have been there all night.

When we came to bat in the 2nd inning, I suggested to the head coach that we empty our bench to allow our underclassmen to finally get some playing time. I was stunned when she refused my request. She stated that our younger players were not "ready" to play in a real game. Mind you, we had yet to win a game the entire season.

I decided to take matters into my own hands. Taylor led off at the top of the 2nd inning, and I told her to draw a walk and then steal second base. However, in doing so, she should fake an injury so that she could be replaced by a younger player.

Taylor did exactly as I instructed. When she slid into second base, she screamed out in pain while grabbing her "injured" ankle. She looked like a fish flopping out of water as she rolled in the dirt. Two of her teammates proceeded to carry her to our bench.

Amazingly, our head coach panicked. "What are we going to do if Taylor can't play?" I assured her that our lead was safe and our younger players were ready to play.

Taylor's replacement eventually got two plate appearances and even got a hit. The highlight of that season was her Mom hugging me after the game, thanking me for giving her daughter the opportunity to play. Everyone but our head coach had long figured out that Taylor had faked her injury.

I had the most fun coaching Travis. When he was in first grade, he expressed an interest in playing tee ball. I expected he would bring registration papers home from school. On the day I signed up our men's team for another year of softball, I asked our league director when I should expect the papers from the school. He informed me that tee ball registration had been completed. Travis either never received the papers or lost them.

The league director then said that if I were to volunteer to coach a team, Travis could play for me. That is how my Little League coaching career began. I had never played tee ball and did not know the rules. At our coaches meeting, the tee ball director told me to simply teach them what base to run to. Heck, I could do that! Fast forward to our first game and our first batter. Little sweet Emily hit a groundball to the shortstop and proceeded to run straight to third base! I am proud to say that we got better as the season progressed.

The real fun started when I started coaching in the Rockville Boys Baseball Pee Wee Division. Who would have guessed our team sponsor would be Optimist? Things had changed over the years. Fewer kids were playing baseball. When was the last time you saw two kids playing catch in their front yard or playing a pickup game of baseball down in the schoolyard? Optimist players were no longer restricted to kids from

Twinbrook Elementary. Team members now lived throughout Rockville.

Travis was a lefty, tall and skinny like his old man. His nickname was "Wild Thing" because he threw extremely hard. You just didn't know where his pitch would go. We would bring Travis into games once the outcome had been decided. He learned how to pitch through trial and error, sometimes striking out three batters in a row, sometimes beaning the same number of hitters.

During my first year coaching Pee Wee, our team was undefeated as we advanced to the best of three city championship. Rules to the games had changed since I had played. Games now lasted six innings. Pitchers could not pitch more than three innings per game nor pitch in consecutive games. I often found myself thinking about how these changes would have helped me when I had played.

But the biggest change involved our schedule. The season started in late April and ended by mid-June. This was so that parents could take their kids on summer vacations. Only players who signed up for travel teams played in the summer anymore.

I served as our pitching coach, and in addition to Travis, we had several pitchers who were really good. While most teams were fortunate to have one good starting pitcher, we had four who could start for any team.

Our plan for game one of the city championship was to have our two top pitchers throw three innings apiece. With a win, this would allow us to have our next two starters available to pitch the deciding second game.

Our plan worked to perfection. We led 6-3, entering the top of the sixth. After retiring the first two batters he faced, our second pitcher walked three consecutive batters, bringing the lead run to the plate. Our pitcher was visibly tired and distressed. If he did not complete the game, we would be forced to turn to our third starter for relief. As a result, that third pitcher would be unavailable for game two.

I called timeout and went to the mound. Our pitcher looked extremely nervous as sweat poured down his face. I took the ball from his glove and looked him straight in the eye. I told him that I could care less if we won. After all, it was just a game. But his mother had instructed me to tell him not to bother coming home if he didn't strike the batter out. He burst out laughing as I gave him the ball and returned to our dugout. He proceeded to strike out the batter to end the game. We clinched the series with our game two victory, with our next two pitchers tossing three innings each.

Following our undefeated season, our coaching staff was chosen to manage the Rockville team in the Washington Metropolitan Tournament. This was the same tournament that

I had played in years before that ended quickly after two blowout losses.

A two-day tryout was held to pick our 15-man roster. Just as when I played, many of the players were sons of coaches, and many were not very good. When we decided to include five of our own players on the final roster; shit hit the fan.

Many coaches criticized our decisions. Most felt that a single player from every team should be chosen. Since Rockville never fared well in this tournament, we felt our choices were the right ones. After all, our players were used to winning.

Eventually, our head coach bowed to the pressure. For game one of the double-elimination tournament, he decided to start just one of our players. The other four would not play in the game. It was a decision we would soon regret.

Our opponent was Burtonsville, Maryland, and they simply kicked our ass. They were a well-rounded team with sound pitching, excellent defense, and good hitters throughout their lineup. Following our 12-1 thumping, we were upset. After all, this was our first loss all season. From then on, we decided to play our best nine players, including all five of our own.

We proceeded to win most of our games handily. Travis started in centerfield and played well, showing off his strong arm by throwing out two base runners at home plate. No one could recall the last time Rockville won the tournament. So when we advanced to the championship game, it was big news. Our opponent was, once again, Burtonsville.

I was highly confident of our chances for victory. Burtonsville had not seen our real team, and I suspected they would be overconfident.

Sure enough, we jumped to a 2-0 lead in the top of the first. Burtonsville appeared rattled. We had them just where we wanted them. The victory was ours!

Fast forward to the sixth and final inning. Burtonsville now led 10-2! The simple fact was that we were matched against a juggernaut.

Travis led off the last inning by drawing a walk. I was coaching first base. As Travis reached the base he turned to me and asked if he should steal second base. Well, there were two reasons why that was a bad idea, First, we trailed by eight runs! It would be foolish to make the first out on the base paths. Second, the Burtonsville catcher was outstanding. He had an extremely strong throwing arm that was even better than my old teammate Andy.

I told Travis to just take it a base at a time. Do not do anything stupid. We would try to put together a rally.

On the very next pitch, Travis wandered off the base too far, and the Burtonsville catcher threw down on a pickoff attempt. Travis dived back to the base.

To this day I insist that Travis was safe. He beat the throw to the bag. Barely. Unfortunately, the base umpire did not have the proper angle to see the play and called Travis out.

I looked down at Travis as he lay in the dirt. He looked like Pigpen from Peanuts. If it had been a close game, I would have aired my grievance to the umpire. Instead, I bent down, looked Travis squarely in the eye and said, "Get your dumb ass off the field." My kid had just embarrassed me in front of 200 people.

With the passage of time, I have embellished this story. I have constantly changed the attendance figures for the game. Just last week, Travis asked me to tell his coworker how many people were in attendance. "Easily 75,000," I said. To his credit, Travis never seems to tire of my yarn.

The following year, the league instituted a slaughter rule. A game would end if a team was ahead by ten or more runs by the end of the fourth inning. Many of our games ended in that manner. The one game I circled on our schedule was St. Mary's. Unfortunately, we did not play them the previous season. Once again, they were one of the best teams in the league. Could I finally get redemption for me and my F.O. Day teammates from 20 years ago?

Since most of our games were rarely contested, I always stressed the need to express good sportsmanship to our opponents. Once we had a significant lead, I would cease our running game and empty our bench. I am almost ashamed to admit that St. Mary's was the one game that I would probably have ignored such sportsmanship.

While the game was never in doubt, St. Mary's played hard and well. I grudgingly respected them for once again fielding an excellent team. But after our 8-1 victory, I did alter one post-game tradition that we followed. I kept the game ball for myself. For the past 30 years it has been displayed in my trophy case, a display of admiration for my former teammates and coaches.

Chapter 45
Thank You, Facebook

Throughout the course of this writing, I've thought of my old coach Wayne Kline. I had not seen or talked to him in over 50 years and had no idea whether he was even alive. My biggest hope was that I would find him one day and talk about these stories I have shared. I wanted nothing more than to let Wayne know how much he meant to me and that the two seasons we were together had provided me with a lifetime of memories.

I turned to Facebook to find my missing coach. I posted a query on the Richard Montgomery High School Facebook page asking for anyone's help in my search. Within hours, I received multiple responses.

My final chapter is dedicated to those Richard Montgomery alumni who provided me with the information I was looking for. Their efforts have provided me with closure needed to complete my story.

Chapter 46
Rest in Peace

Coach Wayne passed away from cancer in 2005. For 20 years, he ran Rolling Stone Press in Georgia, where he became known as the Johnny Appleseed of fine art lithography in Atlanta. During that time, he produced 150 prints by 65 local, regional, and nationally known artists.

Artists had a close connection to Wayne. "He allowed the artists to express themselves," said Annette Cone-Skelton, director of the Museum of Contemporary Art in Georgia. "He pushed them to go that one step further. That is one of the marks of a real master printer."

Using his VA benefits to attend art school, Wayne fell in love with lithography while studying at the Atlanta College of Art, and earning his master's degree at Florida State University. He later attended a prestigious course for master printers at Tamarind Institute in New Mexico.

Wayne's obituary stated that his own lithography generally took a back seat to printing for others, but his attendance at the Caversham Center for Artists and Writers in South Africa and a residency in Belgium sponsored by the King Baudouin Foundation provided him time for his own work.

Said former Atlanta artist Barbara Schreiber, "Wayne was part missionary, part therapist, part coach." Her description made me smile.

Wayne never lost his love for baseball. He became a huge fan of the Atlanta Braves and was incredibly proud of his son, who played baseball at Appalachian State University. Wayne attended many of his games.

His obituary details his joining the Marines out of high school and being discharged after suffering his war wound. While the obituary states that he spent a few desultory years upon his discharge from the Marine Corp I just hope he knew how much my teammates and myself admired him.

Wayne was only 55 years old at the time of his death. I hope one day to provide his son with a copy of this book.

Conclusion

I would be amiss, and I'm certain she would be peeved if I finished my book and failed to mention the most important person in my life, my beautiful wife Lorri. Besides, I'm going to need her support to get this book published!

We first met in 1985 while working at the Reston Twin Theatres. I was 25, and Lorri was 19. I was separated from my first wife and working full time for the Red Cross. Combat Sports was about to go belly up, and my security career was about to begin. I took a part-time job at the theatre for extra income. Travis was just two years old.

Lorri and I dated for a couple of months. She was just a fun person to be around, especially the time I had to pick her up from the ladies' room floor while she laughed hysterically after accidentally eating a hash-glazed brownie. And just like today, her beautiful eyes made my heart melt. I fell in love with her but also suspected that everything I was dealing with would overwhelm most 19-year-olds. She saw my reluctance to pursue a full-blown relationship as indifference. So one day, she handed me a Dear John letter. While I was stunned, I should have been grateful. I am quite confident that if we fast-forwarded that moment to the present day, she would have dumped me by text instead.

As my second marriage was ending, Lorri and I reconnected via

Facebook. She too had experienced failed marriages. We dated for a few years before marrying in 2019.

We are the proud parents of five and the grandparents of seven. We find nothing more enjoyable than spending time with our family. In fact, some might consider us anti-social. After all, is it normal for one to drop onto the floor to avoid detection whenever the front doorbell rings?

Despite two strikes from previous marriages, I have hit a home run with Lorri. We love each others company. At least she hasn't wished me dead yet. Her previous ex wasn't as lucky. I have told her that our love will last forever and that we'll never have to go through a dreadful divorce again. Besides, I have already informed her that I will bury her body in the backyard if it came down to that. But I am fairly certain our dogs would just dig her up.

I never became a professional baseball player. My dream of one day pitching for my beloved Pittsburgh Pirates ended before I even entered high school. And thanks to Ted, my crippled knee prevented me from serving in the military. However, I continue to enjoy substitute teaching. Spending time with elementary school kids keeps my mind young as my body grows old.

As a result of all my knee surgeries, my days of playing sports are long past. My daily exercise consists of walking my Silver Lab, Neville. On occasion, we will walk down to a field near my house. I will let him off his leash and toss a tennis ball over and over again. Neville tirelessly chases each throw and returns the ball every time. My mind often reflects back to the days of my youth and my teammates and coaches from our seasons together. I miss each and every one of them. Even Davey. When my shoulder and elbow begin to ache, Nev and I return home to collapse on the couch.

Afterward

Rodney Miller

Dad always said he intended to be the oldest surviving WWII vet. But as his health declined, he did the next best thing. He died on July 4, 2007. He was 82 years old.

Jean Miller

Mom would blame Wayne until her dying day for not knowing I would exceed my pitching innings limit against Optimist. For 21 years, she served as our scorekeeper when Butch and I played softball in the Rockville Men's Softball League. She took immense pride in always keeping a clean scorebook. Mom never forgave Mrs. Richardson for blaming me for losing the championship game to St. Marys. Mom died in 2017 at 88, still a devout baseball fan and a hater of the Washington Redskins.

Cathy Miller

Now lives in Pennsylvania with her three ugly dogs. After a long career as a drug distribution manager for clinical studies she is now semi-retired and enjoys working at her local Cracker Barrel. At the time of the publishing of this book, my sister has had no additional amputations. But give her time. Meanwhile, I avoid seeing any doctor she has been a patient of.

Butch Miller

Retired as director of his repository and moved to South Carolina. He became a die-hard conservative Republican, making him a fun target for his liberal-minded younger brothers.

A Miller Brothers road trip was planned in 2015 from Charles Town, West Virginia, to Seattle, Washington, to visit my grandchildren. The one stipulation was that no one could talk politics. Unfortunately, Ted suffered a stroke, and the road trip was canceled. Upon further reflection, it was just as well that the trip was canceled. Ted figured we would have only lasted a couple hundred miles before politics would be discussed. Butch would have only gotten pissed off and demanded to be dropped off at the nearest airport, leaving us to continue our trip by ourselves.

Ted Miller

Big Brother #2 retired years ago and, despite his stroke, walks 15,000 steps every day. He has also become a fanatical reader, averaging a book a day for ten consecutive years. How messed up is that? Is it really necessary to read 128 books on General George Armstrong Custer or 93 books on the Battle of Midway?

Barb Dillon

Barb retired in 2018 following a 40-year career in medical transcription. She and her husband Bill moved to Georgia in 2022. I have not seen her in a few years, but I hope one day to visit. Perhaps I will take her to her favorite Georgian restaurant unless, of course, it's a Chinese place.

Andy Thompson

Stopped playing baseball before entering high school. Despite his large size, he was the best catcher I ever saw. Following graduation, we lost touch. The last I heard, he became an auto mechanic and operated his own shop in Bethesda, Maryland. My son, Travis Andrew Miller, was named in his honor.

David Moody

Never played baseball again. Instead, he returned to his bowling league. His absence was certainly felt on our team. Whenever I see professional bowling on television, I pause to see who the bowlers are. I always wondered if David moved up from duckpin bowling to the big time of the Professional Bowlers Association.

Timmy Wise

Timmy and I drifted apart once we reached junior high. I

occasionally played basketball against him in the Twinbrook gym and later faced him in the adult softball league. He is now retired and living in South Carolina.

Davey Richardson

I have never forgiven "Hands of Stone" for costing us the league championship. I had a World History class with him during my senior year in high school. I took great pleasure in reminding him every day how he cost us the title.

Larry "McBoob"

I never completed the manuscript for Larry's Song, but I still have time to win that Pulitzer Prize. Larry moved to Texas to be near his family in the early 1990s. He later suffered from Alzheimer's and died in 2012 at the age of 62. Until his dying day, I wonder if he kept his subscription to Highlights.

Jerry "Duck" Gavin

I will always remember him for dropping the fly ball that cost us redemption against St. Mary's. I will also remember him for always having a smile on his face. I was saddened to learn just recently that Duck passed away in 2021. He was just 60 years old.

Coach Gerald Wright

Stopped coaching baseball after my final year. He retired and became active in his Neighborhood Watch Program. Neighbors appreciated him yelling at drivers for driving too fast in their neighborhood. Coach Wright died in 2021 at the age of 79, no doubt never forgiving my brother for tearing up his lineup.

Bobby Puhl

I never played against him again. I do not know where he is today, nor do I care. But on behalf of my F.O. Day teammates, if I saw him today, I would tell him to shove his gold cleats up his ass.

Acknowledgements

Writing this book completed a dream I have possessed for over 50 years. Perhaps now I can finally stop thinking about losing that championship series. But I doubt it.

There are many people, past and present, who made this book possible. Thank you all for the memories you've provided.

To Mom and Dad - I miss you dearly every day. Thank you for your love and support and for instilling in me the importance of a strong work ethic while understanding a sense of humor is a good thing too.

To my siblings Butch, Ted, Barb, and Cath - No one could ask for better brothers and sisters, even those who tortured the hell out of me when I was just an innocent child. These stories are as much yours as mine. Special thanks to Big Bro # 2 for helping edit this book. I bet you thought your days of the red pen were over, huh?

To my former F.O Day teammates who are at the heart of this story - I wish you all have lived happy and wonderful lives. Even Davey.

To my former coaches, Wayne and Gerald, and to those I did not mention by name - In your own unique ways, you each helped shape me into becoming the man I am. Semper Fi.

To all my former co-workers at Flow Labs, the American Red Cross, and McKesson - Whether it was adding passages to Larry's Song, cooking Maryland blue crabs in the autoclave, or perfecting our wrestling moves, those were some of the best years of my life.

To all my former softball buddies, Juan, JP, Rick, Keith, DT, Roger, Louis, Mike, Dave (where are you?), JT, Brian, Hodo, Pat, Spud, Bob, Jim, Hugh, Vinnie, Bill, Terry, Charlie, and others - Thank you for an amazing 21 seasons of fun. Imagine just how good we would have been had many of us waited until AFTER the game for liquid refreshments?

To Mr. John Cousins, 6th grade teacher, Twinbrook Elementary School- Thank you for making me do my best and understanding the value of a strong education. I hope I made you proud.

To Dr. Thomas Thiele, substitute teacher, Richard Montgomery High School - You were the inspiration for me to become a substitute teacher myself. I only wish I could have told you that in person.

To every security officer I ever employed at the Red Cross or Fort Detrick - Thank you for your dedicated service, but frankly, I hope I never see most of you again.

To Toni and Larry - Thank you for accepting me into your family. Your love and support got me through some difficult times. It's a shame Larry scared the hell out of me back in 1985, otherwise, you guys might have gained a wonderful son-in-law sooner rather than later. So, when can I expect more ribs and stuffing?

To my children, Travis, Taylor, Zac, Mollie, and Casey - The greatest job (and sometimes the hardest too) is being a Dad. I have tried my best. And in those instances where I have failed, blame your Mother.

Finally, to my beautiful grandchildren Chloe, Maddie, Cameron, "Whatsa," Tommy, Natalie, and Charlie - You are all perfect in my eyes. Don't let your parents tell you otherwise.

About the Author

Tom Miller is a retired security professional and current elementary school substitute teacher. He lives in Ashburn, Virginia, with his wife Lorri and pets Sam, Neville, Maggie, Bean, LooLoo, and LeeLoo. This is his first book.

Made in United States
Orlando, FL
09 April 2024

45638677R00114